PHYSICIAN UNDERDOG

LEVERAGING THE UNDERDOG MENTALITY TO
MOVE FORWARD

NAVIN GOYAL M.D.

AMPLIFY NG, LLC.

Published by Amplify NG, LLC.

Cover design by Adam Lehman

Author's photograph by Niraj Shekhar

Contributors to this book: Tarun Bhalla M.D., Leah Houston M.D., Tran T. Huynh D.O., Shikha Jain M.D., Wendy Kirkland M.D., Ketan Kulkarni M.D., Marshall Kuremsky M.D., Ajay Satyapriya M.D., and Kellie L. Stecher M.D.

LOUD Capital can bring the author to your live event. For more information or to book an event, visit our website at www.physicianunderdog.com.

This book is dedicated to my DAD.
He worked very hard while using all the human capabilities of being kind,
welcoming, and positive. I will always miss him and be inspired
by him forever.

CONTENTS

Author's Note   vii

1. What is an Underdog   1
2. The Physician Underdog   13
3. Becoming an M.D.   24
4. Finding Inspiration   45
5. A Shift in Mindset   54
6. Operation Hustle   69
7. Let's Get LOUD   82
8. The Empowered Physician   110
9. Get Moving   122

   Recommended Resources   141
   Acknowledgments   145

AUTHOR'S NOTE

Writing down thoughts was therapeutic, and it created a lot of clarity in a mind full of ideas and experiences. It took my memories, my actions, and my emotions and connected them to a journey. While writing is therapeutic, I never would have thought that I would write anything unsolicited. It wasn't my thing, yet here we are. A series of events led me here. That's life, and they say you never know where it's going to take you. But life itself doesn't actually take you anywhere, it's the steps you take in anticipation or in a reaction to life that create changes. Taking small steps forward can be a game-changer, and I am grateful for the opportunity to take you along on my journey.

Why a Book?

While an experienced medical professional, moving into investment and entrepreneurship was an exciting and very new path for me. It was uncharted territory, it was a whole new language and group of people, and it was an awakening. After gaining insights, experience, and confidence, I was motivated to share what I learned with my colleagues. I began by speaking directly to other

professionals with the goal of opening their minds to explore all of
the various ways beyond health care by which we can contribute
to society and utilize and expand our skills. When I speak, I begin
by sharing my early intentions of pursuing a medical education
and then finish with how I arrived at my current concentration as
an entrepreneur and investor. I am grateful for the opportunity to
share the insights I have gained on this journey. I have been told
repeatedly that my story is unique—a "lightbulb" moment for
many—and inspiring. Many have shared that they felt embold-
ened by the conversation and, not surprisingly, many have gone
on to realize their potential as entrepreneurs.

It's important to know who I really am though, and what I
really did. When you look back and see how I took "leaps" and
how I made "big decisions," it's difficult to fathom and it's hard to
relate to. But actually what happened was quite the opposite. It
was many small steps over many days that took this person, me, to
move forward in different ways, which in turn opened up opportunities not only for myself but also for others. My goal is to have
you read this, relate to this, and move forward on your own small
steps. It takes one person and one step, and fortunately, we are all
capable of doing that.

After many conversations similar to the ones that I have
described—with so many people saying that what I shared
inspired them to think bigger, differently, or just surprised them
enough to think out of the box—I felt it would be helpful to collect
the content of my conversations and stories into a book, with the
hope to impact others, and hopefully inspire a few people to think
on a broader scale. Despite my medical background, my life
mission has changed. While still very much a medical professional,
my mission now is to share my experiences as an entrepreneur and
investor, and reach out to others in the medical field and share
innovative ways to fulfill their goals, satisfy their ambitions, and
be of service. It's important to me that the goals are stated and that
this book was written with that intention in mind.

Here's the thing. I know that I'm not alone. I know that when I have conversations about my journey with people, their eyes widen, their heads nod, and their posture straightens. They understand me. They know exactly what I'm talking about, and they want to express their understanding and share their own stories while relating to what I am saying. While I was writing this book, I decided that it wasn't enough to just tell my story and all the obstacles it has entailed, but to share other physicians' stories of adversity, of being an underdog, and the ways in which they overcame those challenges. I thought it would be helpful to drive the point that most of us go through these really stressful and life-changing scenarios together, not individually. That's really the main point here. We are not alone. We deal with a lot of obstacles, and it's about connecting with other people, connecting with their journeys, and applying those experiences and insights to our own lives that will ultimately help us all to move forward. If we can help each other to keep going, keep learning, and keep sharing what happens along the way, we will be better as individuals and as a community. This is important to me at this stage in my life. I want to keep going. I want to learn more. I want to be better.

This book is one step in fulfilling my goal. I hope you enjoy what I am sharing and that it makes you think a little differently. I hope this information inspires you to explore endless possibilities in the spirit of making the world a much more positive place. There can never be enough positive things we read or hear about, and I hope I have added one more thing to your list.

Why an Underdog?

This book title and the underlying narrative describes the underdog. Why did I want to focus on the underdog? In reflecting on my journey thus far, and the changes I had to make in my life regarding learning and unlearning, I realized that my aspirational career of being a physician ended up placing me in an underdog position. What? How do the word physician and the word underdog get into one sentence? Well, unfortunately, it's where I think the existing state of physicians lies, based on my experience of being inside the system and now being on the outside. Fortunately, there are always things we can do. Always. I will give you some of the background, the current state of physicians, various other industry underdog stories, my story as a physician in clinical medicine to a physician in venture capital, and the benefits that being in an underdog position can produce. There is a different approach that an underdog must take and the pressure can crush you to nothing . . . or it can produce the finest qualities you can exhibit.

 Being an underdog means that you have nowhere to go but up, nothing to prove but everything, and no one to impress but everyone, all of which makes the taste of accomplishment that much sweeter.

— BRIAN PENICK, PARTNER AND CHIEF MARKETING OFFICER AT LOUD CAPITAL

I have personally overcome some obstacles and I am not only excited to share them with you, but I also hope that some of these experiences can lend insight and give you a higher chance of success when overcoming doubt, adversity, or just being in a scenario where you are bet against. I know now that I was the underdog, and chances are (if you are reading along with me) you are in a similar scenario. Calling out the control or lack of control you have is the first step to making progress. This didn't happen overnight and I will share this shift in mindset moving forward in the text. I still consider myself to be in an underdog position and, at this point in my life, I acknowledge that this situation is the fuel that motivates me. I embrace this position vs feeling helpless. This underdog—yes me, the one who never even thought about writing a book and, in fact, despised writing growing up—is driven to utilize education, entrepreneurship, and investing to impact society for the better. I am speaking from experience and not from studying, and I hope that you will create your own experiences and pass along your own lessons.

1

WHAT IS AN UNDERDOG

The underdog has become a big part of my character. It is the source of energy I get when learning something new, the source of energy that motivates me to problem-solve, and it has become my attitude when embracing and accepting that I am different. As a self-acknowledged and consistent underdog, I believe the first step to empowerment is knowing that while from the outside it appears that you have less to work with, actually acknowledging your underdog status helps you discover unrealized and underutilized resources and traits in yourself that have been there from the get-go.

Describing someone as an underdog, in my simple interpretation, is saying that there is unknown potential that can be revealed in perhaps any situation. Now, I happen to be a futuristic type of thinker, one who gets excited about what can be and what is possible. I try to use history, experience, and the wisdom of others as a foundation to look upon and move forward, not as an obstacle to avoid. There is so much untapped potential in people, and the underdog is simply a judgment of what is perceived. In fact, it narrowly describes some external qualities that are readily seen. But, that is not my perception. In my mind, "underdog" is a label that indicates qualities or traits that have not yet been exhibited; a label that would inhibit some while motivating others. The underdog is unproven, but it is how we "underdogs" look to the future. Many of us aren't done yet; we still have time to prove ourselves against the clock. We haven't exhibited traits and qualities where people would bet on us, but that doesn't mean that that potential is not deep inside us or within our minds.

The label of being an underdog, with an enlightened mindset, creates the drive and energy that can turn barriers perceived into ramps to get you launched and move you upward and forward. The underdog exposes unknown potential, which is exciting, not disappointing. It's all about the future. Turning the tables around, the so-called current loser could potentially become the winner. The current disaster may in fact be a blessing. The current label is not a judgment of what you can do today or tomorrow, it's simply an assessment of your past performance. I'm not sure the public's perception has necessarily changed, but I know mine has.

 Really doesn't matter if I lose this fight. Because all I want to do is go the distance.

— ROCKY BALBOA, *ROCKY* (UNITED ARTISTS, 1976)

I am really interested in looking at the traits and obstacles that can push the underdog in a direction that perhaps is more favorable. Favorable can snowball from being bet against into being bet on. I will share a few examples of underdog stories that inspired me and show the resilience and courage of what people can do when challenged. The goal is to showcase how many obstacles were faced and then overcome. Perhaps it's because I have two sisters, a wife, two daughters, and many mothers around me, or maybe it's because I have met many women in medicine and in the entrepreneurial world who have dealt with their own adversity simply by being women. I am more sympathetic as I observe how the world can have such elevated standards for women in the various roles they play. I want to share some stories that I have found of women who have faced obstacles head-on and have over-come and succeeded. I feel their stories are extremely inspiring. I may have some familial awareness, but I feel being a woman in a male-dominated culture can be an underdog story in and of itself. Adding to that the other factors facing every underdog who perse-veres and moves forward . . . they are all stories worth sharing. I found many different stories coming from the world of sports, entrepreneurship, or people just experiencing their lives. These stories have inspired me and I know they will inspire you.

A PHYSICIAN UNDERDOG OVERCOMES

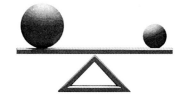

YOU CAN HAVE IT ALL. ISN'T THAT WHAT YOUR PARENTS TOLD YOU while growing up? Well, this is what I tell my children. My young daughter is only four and yes, I want her to "have it all." But what does that really mean?

Especially for women, this illustrious phrase can inflict stress and anxiety. There are sacrifices that any working parent must make, but oftentimes men aren't plagued by the same societal pressures that women face. For example, my husband never gets asked "well who watches your children?" while he is cutting into someone's face. However, as I am deli-cately suturing with 10-0 nylon, my childcare situation seems to be a popular topic of discussion.

Women oftentimes feel the pressure to be able to do "everything" and do it with a smile on their faces. The amount of times that patients make comments about my appearance is astonishing. And I'm not just talking

3

about the popular comment, "you look too young to be a doctor!" My husband never hears "your hair looks good like that" or "I love that necklace on you." Honestly, most of them are compliments, but again, people feel the need to judge me not only on my professional skill but also on how well put together I am. The pressure to BE good, LOOK good, and FEEL good can be overwhelming and it is very prevalent in today's society.

And of course, there is the ever so popular term of "mom guilt." Why have I never heard of "dad guilt"? Because women are expected to be the caregivers and when you aren't the person giving care, you must obviously feel guilty, right? This leaves many women physicians feeling inadequate at home, at work, or both.

Striving to have it all can be exhausting. But striving to be the best version of yourself is much more achievable. Surrounding yourself with people that want to help you achieve this goal is critical. And most importantly, giving yourself some grace is most necessary.

I think the secret to having it all is actually knowing that you can't, and that's ok. It is a game of give and takes. Our careers, families, health, and overall stress levels are not on a straight-line path, and knowing that there will be awesome highs and terrible lows is how we grow. Everyone's term of "having it all" really depends on what makes them happy. Ultimately, striving to do what makes YOU happy is a much better goal than "having it all."

WENDY KIRKLAND M.D.

ONE OF MY FAVORITE UNDERDOG STORIES IS THE ONE OF SARA BLAKELY and her company, Spanx. At the time of this writing, it's already easy to forget where she came from. You have listened to her many interviews, you've seen her products and stores in many geographical areas, and heard her story in the context of great entrepreneurs. But it's really important to know that she was and still is the woman next door. When she began her business, she had never taken a business class and had never worked in fashion or retail. She had been selling fax machines door to door for several years and had a small amount of savings. Then one day, when deciding what to wear to a party, she was trying to avoid any lines from panties or shapers showing through her white pants. So she cut the feet out of her pantyhose, attended the event, and realized that she felt great wearing the adjusted undergarment.

When she had the idea of creating hosiery that was cut off beyond the legs, she got crazy looks and unanswered calls when reaching out for help. After several conversations, and realizing that the hosiery industry was shaped and run predominantly by men, she felt that her perspective may have been more reasonable than initially thought. She trusted her own perspective, which is an obstacle in itself for many of us. She kept moving forward, patented her idea, and had women give their input on feel, size, and shape for her Spanx line. When people say they had to hustle, it could mean that they had to reach out to people and get feedback for their product. That may sound simple, but putting yourself out there and getting criticism on what you believe is something special, regardless of whether you receive a positive or negative response, you learn something. It was a male-dominated industry that women tolerated, and Sara had a lot of courage to build what she thought made sense, despite what the industry around her was saying.

Sara's first big deal was with Neiman Marcus stores. Yes, this is a big deal for any entrepreneur, but the way she made it happen is even better. She cold-called the company for a few days and finally connected with someone. She then told them if they gave her a few minutes of their time, she would fly down to Dallas to show them her product. They said that if she was willing to fly, then the executive would give her ten minutes of her time. When she felt this short meeting wasn't going well, she took the female executive to the bathroom and showed her what her pants looked like with and without her product. (Yes, she asked her to come with her to the bathroom.) That demonstration closed the deal. This is a true story of a brand many of us know, but the way this founder made it happen and the small yet courageous steps she took to move forward, is not just inspirational, it is relatable. The perseverance of this underdog is something to be shared, something to be excited about, and something we can use to arm ourselves moving forward. The perseverance and courage of Sara Blakely are what turned this unknown entrepreneur into a true entrepreneurial role model.

 I think my story says that, when women are given the chance and the opportunity, that we can achieve a lot. We deliver.

— SARA BLAKELY, AMERICAN BUSINESSWOMAN AND
PHILANTHROPIST

Anita Roddick's story is another great tale of an underdog achieving. Roddick was born in England with three other siblings and worked after school and on weekends at their family restaurant. She got married in 1970 and, early in their marriage, Anita and her husband ran a bed-and-breakfast lodging combined with a health food restaurant. When her husband wanted to pursue a lifelong dream of riding his horse from Argentina to New York, she began to cook moisturizers in her Brighton, England, home to support her children financially. She also agreed to sell their restaurant in order to finance his trip. Anita was supportive of her husband's goal and admired his determination even with the new financial stress that it brought upon their family.

Anita had experience traveling around the world before she got married and during that time observed people with magnificent skin who were rubbing their bodies with cocoa butter. It opened up her mind to unconventional body care, which became an interest to her. Roddick opened her first Body Shop (a retail store for her signature cosmetic line) without expectations of getting wealthy. She wanted to create a cosmetic line that would use natural ingredients and appeal to consumers who care about the environment. Rather than succumbing to vanity and the marketing strategies of the large cosmetic companies at the time, she utilized low-key marketing, social activism, and consumer education to take The Body Shop[r] from a small-scale company to a massive one. At this writing, The Body Shop is recognized as having helped shape the playbook for the multi-billion, global cosmetic industry. If it isn't obvious, she was a massive underdog. She was a female entrepreneur in a situation where she had to sell products to survive and, at the same time, she was starting a new business in an industry that already had giants with big pockets.

I knew this brand but I didn't know about Anita and I didn't know anything about her story. Now I feel that her courage should be celebrated, and the fact that she humanized our perspective of what a large company makes her story more relatable. We are all just small steps away from building our own paths.

 I started The Body Shop in 1976 simply to create a livelihood for myself and my two daughters, while my husband, Gordon, was trekking across the Americas. I had no training or experience and my only business acumen was Gordon's advice to take sales of £300 a week. Nobody talks of entrepreneurship as survival, but that's exactly what it is and what nurtures creative thinking . . . If I could give one piece of advice to anyone, it's don't obsess with this notion that you have to turn everything you do into a business . . . but if you can create an honorable livelihood, where you take your skills and use them and you earn a living from it, it gives you a sense of freedom and allows you to balance your life the way you want.

— ANITA LUCIA RODDICK (B. 1942–D. 2007), BUSINESSWOMAN,
HUMAN RIGHTS ACTIVIST, AND ENVIRONMENTAL CAMPAIGNER

Oprah Winfrey is a household name that is associated with success and celebrity. She is a strong woman who converses about societal issues on the public stage, and she has built a multi-media empire. What may have gone unnoticed by many, or perhaps forgotten, is that Oprah did not grow up with a strong foundation, nor did she have a leg up to achieve her success. In fact, being a black woman in the U.S. could be characterized as being in a very serious underdog position. Oprah was living in poverty and was switched back and forth between her separated mom and dad. While her mom was busy working, Oprah was sexually abused by men that were trusted by her family members. The continuation of living in urban poverty along with the abuse eventually took a huge toll. Winfrey acted out in a lot of bad ways and, eventually, she was sent to stay with her father (Oprah claims that he saved her life). Her father was very strict and had Oprah focus on studying, structuring her time, and reading books. Winfrey thrived with discipline and became an excellent student. She got involved in multiple clubs at school, including drama and debate, and pursued speaking contests and eventually radio. She was granted a full scholarship to Tennessee State University for winning a speaking contest and eventually got an offer from CBS to do news in Nashville. The rest is history.

A Physician Underdog Overcomes

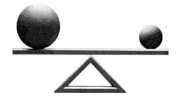

I have wanted to be a doctor since I was eight years old. I successfully completed my medical journey with Medical School, General Surgery Residency, and Breast Surgical Oncology. Fellowship at the age of 34. It took 26 years and a tremendous amount of hard work, grit, resilience, and perseverance to achieve that dream.

Statistically in the U.S., only approximately 36% of physicians are women, approximately 20% of surgeons are women, approximately 17% are Asian, approximately 13% of engineers are women, approximately less than 5% of physicians are Vietnamese, and there are no reliable statistics for LGBTQ+ physicians/engineers because the number is so minute . . . so, as a Vietnamese Asian Woman LGBTQ+ engineer physician surgeon entrepreneur, I am an underdog . . . and I have stood on the shoulders of giants and will continue to help others stand on mine. It takes a village (www.amc.org data reports and news insights).

Tran T. Huynh D.O.

I've always been motivated by an underdog story. In fact, if I had to pick one over the other, I would probably choose the underdog over the "sure thing." There are different things that are appealing about being an underdog vs a favored contender. Being an avid football fan, there is a different level of energy and inspiration that gets behind a team that is viewed as the underdog. The tone, the conversation, the positive qualities—and the potential that the underdog has not yet displayed—all lead to excitement. When talking about a favored team, there is talk on the past performance, how this history would apply to the upcoming game, and there is a focus on the weaknesses and negatives of the underdog team. There is a different mindset when considering the underdog, one that grasps the past as well as the hope and will of the future. And maybe that's it . . . it's about the possibility of overcoming obstacles to get to where you want to be. Exploring these obstacles is an exercise that motivates and energizes me. And this is why I like to discuss my experience and encourage others to embrace the challenges.

In the world of sports, where people are spoken about and celebrated around an event, the word "underdog" is used many times to speak about the work and effort that lead up to the occasion. Tom Brady is an individual who is already known as a legend, but his story is a true underdog story and it includes athleticism, discipline, and leadership. At the 2000 NFL Combine, his performance was rough and the opinions from the scouts were poor. He was slow, didn't leap very far, and overall just seemed to lag. He eventually got drafted into the NFL in the sixth round by the New England Patriots. In the 2001 season, the starting quarterback, Drew Bledsoe, got injured and Tom Brady took over and proved himself to be a strong leader with a powerful arm. That year, with a very dominant defense, they won the Super Bowl, and many folks started to gain respect for the young quarterback. That is a story in itself. As many of us know, he had an incredible run with the Patriots and became a legend after winning three Super Bowl titles in his first four years in the NFL. The story keeps building after Brady spent 20 years with the Patriots, winning six Super Bowl championships, and beating many records. Brady has continued to shock the world as he gets older and continues to win. When he transferred to the Tampa Bay Bucs in 2020, leaving a great coaching staff, culture, and the overall momentum and experience of the Patriots, he became an underdog again by coming into a completely different organization and culture. Despite his age and new team members—and due to his determination, leadership, and athletic abilities—Tampa Bay won a Super Bowl championship in his first year. He has been an underdog in many aspects but continues to inspire by doing what many folks say is impossible. I use this example because Tom Brady has personally inspired me. He has used discipline and hard work to create his own path. That path was questioned many times, and the level of talent and physicality expected in the NFL is so high, yet Brady has defied the odds and inspired the world to question our questioning.

 I'm not a person who defends myself very often. I kind of let my actions speak for me.

— THOMAS EDWARD PATRICK BRADY (B. 1977), AMERICAN
FOOTBALL QUARTERBACK

The realization of being an "underdog" is everything to me. When I say everything, I think when I started to identify myself as an underdog it contributed to who I am today, and to what I have become, and to how I view myself and others in the world. I didn't realize this or even acknowledge it before, but it's something that is crystal clear to me now. It could be my age and being more sentimental, it could be how I see that there are so many different obstacles that people face, or perhaps it's because I have shifted careers and can really take a look from the outside. I realize that being in the underdog position is how I have personally felt all of my life. Perhaps it's one of the reasons I went into medicine—I was seeking to gain winner status, to get out of being an underdog.

Years later, I am disappointed in how I feel physicians are still underdogs. I believe that recognizing that status first and foremost is crucial to real change. Real change for physicians is lifesaving for society. Real change for physicians will not be pretty or easy or smooth. Real change starts with looking in the mirror, then looking outside of medicine and observing how people feel physicians are contributing to the world. My perspective, especially after leaving the practice of medicine and running a business that empowers entrepreneurs and problem-solvers, has been evolving and I feel it needs to be shared.

 Our society and education system pushes us so hard towards a certain path, we don't really discover our true passions and interests until we're in a career.

— RYAN RETCHER, SENIOR PARTNER AND CHIEF OPERATING OFFICER AT LOUD CAPITAL

Once I recognized and acknowledged my underdog status, I knew that I needed to seek out the tools required to turn the state around. I not only wanted to survive, I wanted to thrive. When I look back at my accomplishments and failures (we all have them), the only thing I did consistently was to move forward. I know now that it was the underdog mentality—that all or nothing, let's go mentality—that was propelling me at the time, whether I recognized it or not. My recommendation is to digest, absorb, and hopefully apply some of what I am sharing in this book. My goal is to help others overcome or reimagine the sense of being an underdog. Perhaps many of the ways I looked at and approached my life was in an effort to overcome that perceived underdog status. Years later, as a physician, I am disappointed to observe and confirm how I feel that physicians are in the state of being underdogs. YES! Believe it or not, physicians are underdogs. I believe that recognizing this status, first and foremost, is the crucial first step to making real change. Real change can happen when you realize you aren't alone, that you have the skills and tools to move forward, and that your ability to impact yourself and society as a whole can happen now.

2

THE PHYSICIAN UNDERDOG

The goal of this chapter is not to focus too much on the obvious
state of today's physicians: we are burned out, have high debt, feel
like we are losing control, have allied health providers taking more
responsibility on patient care, reimbursements are going down, we
have less power than before, etc., etc. I do think these things are
really important, but I don't think they are individual problems
that we can bandage. I think they need to be put in the context of a
larger picture examining how we as physicians can take some
philosophical steps forward to allow ourselves to be happier, more
effective, and more impactful—to broaden our scope and become
an even more positive influence on society.

As I see it, in their current state physicians are an intelligent
and capable group of people who train to work within a system
that was not built by them or for them. A system that, like many
businesses, utilizes workers and different levels of labor to care for
patients. The difference is that physicians don't know that they are
laborers in this regard. I will actually repeat this sentence: The way
physicians are positioned in the current hospital system, the results
are that they are being seen and utilized as laborers. Physicians
know that they are driving medical decisions, but they are
deceived in believing that they are contributing to business deci-

sions, such as workflow and staffing. But yes, those decisions are out of their hands. What is more dangerous and/or frustrating? Being a worker and knowing you are one, or being a specialist and not knowing that you are IN FACT, in reality, a worker?

When it comes to the current state of physicians, there is acknowledgment in and out of the field that burnout is not only real, it is actually becoming commonplace and, in fact, it is increasing in numbers. Burnout is described as long-term job-related stress, leading to emotional exhaustion, cynicism, and a lack of interest or sense of accomplishment in doing the work itself. A 2017 survey of physicians found that 43.9% experienced symptoms of burnout. Compared to other working American adults, doctors are more likely to experience professional burnout (a lot of this has to do with the nature of the job—there's a lot at stake, and every second counts). This has led to an increase in mental health disorders among physicians, including 30% higher rates of depression among medical students, a 28% depression rate for resident physicians, and an incredible 43% of practicing physicians experiencing emotional exhaustion. According to studies, the true expense of physician burnout is between $2.6 billion and $6.3 billion per year. This is from the cost of recruiting physicians and then finding a replacement for them when burnout occurs and they either leave or cut back their hours. Turnover is starting to become a problem. Additionally, the U.S. is poised to see a shortage of over 100 thousand physicians by 2032—likely leading to higher rates of burnout and emotional exhaustion.[1]

A DOG'S LIFE

BURNOUT ISN'T A NEW SUBJECT IN THE PHYSICIAN WORLD. IT HAS BEEN growing consistently over the years without any concerted efforts to reduce it or steps taken to address some of the common causes of it. Some of the underlying causes of burnout are the many bureaucratic tasks that have been surrounding the physicians' daily routines and, in fact, have been growing in complexity and time devotion over the years. Some known factors are spending too much time at work or having less efficient days, feeling a lack of respect from administrators and colleagues, and a lack of advanced technologies that save time and work for the practice.

Spending too much time at work is a broad subject that can be due to having more bureaucratic tasks to fulfill, a lack of respect for the physician's time by staff and/or stakeholders, or even a lack of focus to optimize a physician's time. The lack of respect for physicians seems to be the perception that physicians are more workers than thinkers—the direction of the workflow and practice seems not to be controlled by the physician, but by the surrounding administrators and colleagues. Physicians aren't managing the team or the process, rather they are simply a team-mate, similar to many others. The actual coach isn't working on the field and is unseen.

If you compare this to the world outside of healthcare, I would broadly say that technology has allowed people in other fields to work more efficiently, work in a more individualized environment (based on their needs), and has freed up time so users can pursue other activities. The fact that physicians are not experiencing the same benefits is naturally disappointing and I would say even tragic, considering that we are in the modern time of technology, where even the consumer world is being empowered. In summary, physicians feel a lack of control, a lack of respect, and a lack of technological support. As a result, they are experiencing less job satisfaction.

And the burnout trend doesn't seem to be losing steam. There are now books, articles, and seminars devoted to the topic, but considering the prevalence of burnout among physicians, I feel strongly that these are band-aids on a bad bleed. I do appreciate the subject being spoken about, and that it is being discussed amongst various physician groups. Some of the items that are being addressed are meritable, but they require a lot of change. I don't think many physicians really understand how their culture, their structure, and their beliefs affect how limited they are in the ways that they can face obstacles and truly effect change. A group or even an individual can only do a limited amount if they have no real experience in other fields and professional cultures. My goal is to share what I have realized regarding my own intentions and also what I have learned from recent experiences. But to begin, we should discuss the accelerated clarity of the year 2020.

 Wherever the art of Medicine is loved, there is also a love of Humanity.

— Hippocrates, Classical Greek physician

The 2020 pandemic challenged many people, companies, and industries, and it further challenged the healthcare system. It has highlighted the inefficiencies of how the large system can't adapt. It can't provide the basic needs of the workers in the system and the patients that need help. Equally important, this health crisis highlighted the culture and attitude of how physicians have low value in the medical system. Perhaps this was needed to wake up the field of medicine to the lack of access to protective equipment, the lack of support when needed, and the lack of voice when medical expertise was called upon to help guide the country . . . they were all examples of the lack of reach and respect physicians have in the current healthcare system. It's not one decision or one item that physicians should focus upon. Rather, I am encouraging physicians to take a holistic view when approaching obstacles such as those currently being faced during the pandemic. Remember, physicians spend a lot of time and money to get to their position, which brings another factor to the table: physician debt.

There is data that supports how much time and training a physician goes through, all while accumulating extreme debt. According to a recent AAMC report, *Physician Education Debt and the Cost to Attend Medical School: 2020 Update*, 73% of students graduate with debt. And while that percentage has decreased in the last few years, those who do borrow for medical school face big loans: the median debt was $200,000 in 2019. The average four-year cost for public school students is $250,222. For private school students, the cost is $330,180.[2]

A Physician Underdog Overcomes

I AM A PHYSICIAN, A CLINICIAN-RESEARCHER, A SCIENTIST, A PASSIONATE entrepreneur, an ardent advocate of financial literacy and independence with alternative income streams, an avid learner, a traveler, a photographer, an artist (and art enthusiast and antique collector), and a music buff. However, in 2017–2018, I found myself burnt out. I had a growing family and a supportive spouse. I was in my first permanent home. My career was thriving with a very successful research and academic program, and I was climbing the academic ladder. I was working at least 60–70 hours per week. I was feeling tired all the time and found myself distressed and angry many times for petty reasons. I was feeling that I wasn't enough!

While I worked extremely hard during the previous four years in my attending role (after 14 years of training), I realized that a range of limitations and challenges, including red tape, system issues, and politics, exist along the traditional pathways of medicine . . . and I was in the middle of it all. I was wondering if medicine by itself would be fulfilling enough in the long run, but I didn't see any easy solutions. I tried to reach out to friends and colleagues and saw that people, associates, and experts from all walks of life, regardless of the stage of their career and their titles, faced similar issues and were often themselves burnt out.

They were unhappy; however, there were no systematic solutions. People didn't even really want to talk about what they were experiencing for the risk of stigma. One was expected to just put up with it and suck it up. I also sought mentorship, but it was only partially helpful. I heard statements like "this is not an office job, this work is 24/7, you are expected to do this, all academic work happens on evenings and weekends."

Things got worse. While my family continued to grow and I had even more responsibilities outside of work, I faced more challenges in and around the workplace, including office politics. I also faced challenges related to the workplace culture, the plausibly inadequate recognition of diversity and equity, and even faced hard situations through no fault of my own. It was abundantly clear that things could not continue the way they were and I really needed to figure things out. Externally it might have seemed that I was very successful and thriving, but that was certainly not the case. I was not happy.

I realized that I had put most of my passions on the back burner during the long training years, and again over the last few years. As well, I realized that physicians aren't usually well versed in business and finance and often shy away from excellent money management. Fortunately, with the help of one of my core mentors, I was able to enroll in a three-year longitudinal leadership training program. It was a complete game changer and revamped my thinking and perspective. I also had the opportunity to develop my leadership and communication skills and participate in a number of national and international societies, committees, and opportunities. Recently, I obtained an executive leadership certificate.

Around 2016, I started training myself in finance and did some individual investing for a few years. I also expanded to some active and passive real estate investments. Since then, I have taken real control of my finances and now advise friends and colleagues widely on the topic. We also launched a financial mini-MBA at our local medical school.

That said, I still felt that I needed to find and connect with "my own tribe." Thus evolved my vision to connect, network, and collaborate with like-minded individuals who are interested in mastering their own lives and destinies. With a few other colleagues, I co-founded "thrive Rx," which is run by physicians for physicians and emphasizes how to use ancient and modern wisdom to thrive and avoid burnout.

My academic program and medical practice are busier than ever before. With my recently found awareness of myself and my intentional behavior, the burnout is gone. While I still have many miles to go, I feel that I am thriving! I'm sure that if I can achieve this, you can too.

KETAN KULKARNI M.D.

—————

THE BOTTOM LINE

WHILE PHYSICIANS CONTINUE TO GRADUATE WITH EXTREME LEVELS OF debt, they are doing so at a much greater cost than they once did. In 2019, the payment for physician services, which is a complex formula developed by Medicare to determine physician reimbursement, was $36.0391 paid per unit of work, slightly lower than the rate in 1998. This has remained relatively flat for more than two decades, despite general inflation of more than 50% and a large increase in the cost of living during the same period. Had the conversion factor simply been indexed to inflation, physicians would be earning over $57 per unit of work today.[3] Combine this with growing rates of physician burnout and a large increase in mental health issues, it is clear why there are fewer people today opting to pursue a career as a physician. More and more people are now pursuing specialized fields such as nurse practitioner (NP) or physician assistant (PA).[4]

When it comes to advanced practice providers (APPs), such as nurse practitioners and physician assistants, there seems to be a constant power struggle between being managed by physicians in patient care, and practicing independent of physician input or overview. I understand the amount of training and expertise that physicians hold for optimal patient care, but I also understand that there aren't enough physicians to serve all patients' needs. In a perfect world (which is how I start with my problem-solving initiatives), physicians would be able to create a system that manages patient care in every corner of the healthcare system and non-healthcare system whenever it comes to people's health. Physicians would be involved in the policy and the execution and would be constantly modifying their skills as information and research changed. In this way, they would be able to adapt to the most effective and economical ways to help people thrive in their health. What we have now is completely the opposite of what I think the perfect world should look like. We have physicians involved mainly in direct patient care while many non-physicians are shaping our systems and all aspects of healthcare. While many patients aren't being served and the need to take care of them is crucial, there are many other careers that have started (for example, allied health professionals) to fulfill the demand. The demand is there and different states and regulatory bodies are allowing allied practitioners to have more rights to fulfill it, which is slowly putting physicians in a difficult position.

Physicians are frustrated with needing to be experts in their field, while slowly the standards for seeing patients are lowering. You don't have to have a medical degree to diagnose, treat, and prescribe medicine anymore (it does vary from state to state), and this has caused friction in the medical community. This friction is understandable and it's going to be a continuous power struggle if things continue on their current course. Physicians are feeling that they aren't helping shape the provider's responsibilities and the processes in which they have input. Once again, physicians worked hard to get to a level of expertise with the expectation that they would manage patient care, yet it seems that a number of alternative healthcare professionals are slowly growing to fulfill the demand, without direction from physicians.

In summary, the work and effort it takes to become an expert are now being put into question as decisions are being made within and beyond medical systems. If experts can't be in charge of influencing policy and practice, then we are doomed from the beginning. Physicians have worked hard to get to where they are professionally. It's up to us physicians to ensure that we are in control. We also need to acknowledge that there is a whole system of people, including APPs, that must be utilized to ensure that access to care is addressed in a practical manner.

But the advantage comes with a disadvantage. . .

The advantage is that we have the skills and knowledge as individuals in comparison to many others, and we have the capability to do anything on which we set our minds. Yes, individually, we are experts in healthcare for people, and we have proven this to ourselves and to others in our field, and as we have equally shown our ability to learn and incorporate new information and utilize it in an ethical process. However, if we rest on our laurels and think that this knowledge and capability will convert to leading policy and influencing other fields that involve patient care, we are far from the truth. There are many in our physician community that not only feel threatened by APPs, but are not even strategically aligned with other physicians on what we believe we can do to be effective. That's probably not unusual to a small, special group of people who are extremely busy with their primary duty, which is to take care of patients, but it calls for us to step back, figure out our end goals, and take steps to fulfill those goals. I see a lot of short-term emotions and distractions from physicians that cause friction towards APPs and policymakers. But we don't have the time, numbers, or the energy to acknowledge and address the need for more hands-on patient care.

A Physician Underdog Overcomes

I think like a lot of us, it's hard to call myself an underdog based on where I am in life now, especially as so many around the world struggle just to keep a job. But I need to remember all those times where my life story didn't seem so promising or go as planned.

Back in high school, I had done well as an athlete. However, I got denied by multiple big-name colleges (Ivy League) and in my mind had to settle for my state university—Strike 1. In college, I struggled my first year and left premed for a while because of my grades. I had to learn that becoming a doctor might not be in my future despite my desire to be one—Strike 2. After med school, I had set my mind on certain residency programs. I luckily got a spot but only on my fourth choice. I didn't feel so lucky at the time—Strike 3.

I used to feel inadequate because the expectations I had for myself didn't work out as I had planned. This made me feel like I didn't belong at times. What I have realized, though, is that those unexpected scenarios actually gave me strength. It's easy to keep grinding and moving forward when things go your way, but the real test is to use those unexpected scenarios to show you who you really are.

I think all of us feel like underdogs at times, but it's our tenacity and perseverance that make us one no longer.

Ajay Satyapriya M.D.

WE NEED ALL PHYSICIANS TO EMBRACE THE NEED, INFLUENCE THE need, and manage the need from a leadership perspective, not from a shortsighted strategy, but from a higher-level strategy. But, here is the disadvantage: we don't have a plan and we haven't been taught or told to think this way. We need to give ourselves permission to step back, know with confidence we can handle and control any situation, and move forward with a united plan.

(1):https://etactics.com/blog/physician-burnout-statistics
(2):https://www.aamc.org/news-insights/7-ways-reduce-medical-school-debt
(3):https://bulletin.facs.org/2019/09/medicare-physician-payment-on-the-decline-its-not-your-imagination
(4):https://www.aapa.org/news-central/2019/11/pas-tied-for-7th-on-list-of-fastest-growing-professions/

3

BECOMING AN M.D.

My goals and dreams weren't radically different from a lot of other Indian kids growing up in the United States: Go for a profession that will give you a stable career and minimal headaches of employment. Go for something that is ambitious and also a respected profession in the community. The overlapping theme of many of these conversations ended up pointing to the field of medicine. Although some people may not feel as much of the respect factor nowadays in the U.S., a physician, in general, is still a very respected professional, individual, and valuable member of any community around the world.

Growing up in an Indian household, there were not too many rules in my house on academic guidance, except to just study your butt off to get the best grades. Get good grades and good things will follow. My parents came from India in the '60s and like many immigrant families, stayed disciplined while navigating a completely new environment and culture. They dealt with many forms of adversity, including racism, financial challenges, and integrating into a whole new culture. These adversities solidified their determination to help their children avoid such challenges. They knew that going into a medical profession would give them individual credibility and would perhaps give their children an easier life than what they had experienced. That seems more of a parental aspect and, in reflection, as I am now a parent and can only imagine the challenges of immigrating to a new country, especially in the 1960s, I have a much deeper understanding of their goals.

 Immigrant parents dream that their children will find a place in their new home, and they willingly suffer hardships in service to that dream. That was certainly true of my parents.

— Gene Luen Yang, American cartoonist

Getting to my pathway and perspective growing up, it seemed pretty straightforward. As my parents raised me to be hard-working and prioritize school over anything else, I pretty much followed that route with minimal resistance. I had a focused goal: do well in school. As I did the usual studious routine, I started to have an interest in science and math—not too unusual for a first-generation Indian! That being said, I continued to take science-based courses and, somehow, I decided I wanted to be a doctor even while I was still a kid. I always saw the field as a challenge to get into, but I wanted to help people. I saw physicians as extremely intelligent people doing heroic things for others on a daily basis. I also wanted to get into a stable and financially successful field. I definitely saw physicians as getting the respect that didn't seem to be present in other fields.

I didn't know a lot of other professional fields, aside from seeing doctors in the community and watching my dad go to work as an engineer. Sometimes my dad explained his work but it just seemed a little foreign to me. In fact, when I would visit his work once in a while, he would be excited for me to meet his close colleagues and then hit up lunch with him. The focus was on him and his routine over the content of his work, so at these times I never really asked more or dug further into the work he was doing. He was also an engineer who designed many projects that he most likely knew were too high-level and/or complicated for me! Either way, there wasn't anything memorable in that field to turn my consideration to anything outside of medicine. Medicine seemed like a good goal and, since I liked science, I didn't explore or entertain learning about many other things.

Retrospectively, I realize that this wasn't an ideal mindset— while being focused and driven by a single goal is noteworthy, I think learning about other fields, industries, and businesses can give a person a more comprehensive view of what other jobs are like. Being in grade school and even college didn't exactly take me into the trenches of various jobs, but perhaps a curiosity into other areas would have given me more exposure than I had at that time. That being said, I was young and not even thinking about an actual job, rather my mind was set on more of a goal—a "what do you want to be when you grow up" kind of thing.

As college came along I planned on doing a science major and pursuing getting into medical school. I worked hard and was pretty disciplined to get good grades. Even though I wanted to live on campus like a lot of other kids, my parents told me to commute from home for two reasons. The Ohio State University, which was a twenty-minute drive from my house to campus, was so close that it would be a waste of money to live there. They didn't have money to spend on on-campus housing unless necessary, and they knew I was embarking on a long and expensive academic track. The second reason, which I feel was the larger focus, was that if I lived on campus my grades would be at a higher risk. Distractions from other people and things were a concern and my parents felt my living at home would give them a better chance at keeping an eye on my progress. I kicked and I screamed. I felt that I was totally missing out on the college life experience. I wasn't happy about it but I stuck to the plan (I guess I had no other option) and put my head down to do well academically. In my third year of college, after proving my ability to be disciplined and perform well, and after a lot of back and forth with my parents on how I wanted an on-campus experience, I was given the go-ahead and moved on campus. In retrospect, I wanted the freedom of living on campus, but I also knew how much money it cost my parents to do so, costing money that they had saved over a long period of time. I knew I was going to do well by them, but these thoughts were going through my mind as I argued my side of the story. I was betting on myself and I think this power of self-belief should be discussed more.

A PHYSICIAN UNDERDOG OVERCOMES

IMAGINE THAT YOU'RE LIVING OUT YOUR CHILDHOOD DREAM. EXACTLY as you saw it unfolding. And by that, I mean the career and the path and the thing that you set out to do when you were just a teenager. You didn't know it at the time, because you didn't have perspective—but your family influences, and the things other people told you, all kind of naturally geared and pushed you toward becoming a physician.

Imagine further . . . . that not only did you always know you wanted to be a physician, you knew exactly what specialty tugged at your heart-strings. You knew exactly the kind of doctor you wanted to become. So you channeled all of your energy, focus, and drive toward making that happen. It needed all of your grit because the journey was long and ardu-ous. You never looked at it that way, a long journey to endure, because all that mattered was arriving at the finish.

Now imagine . . . you have arrived. Boom. No more rungs on the ladder to climb. Just a few more standardized tests, to earn a few more credentials and board certifications, and then after that, welcome your real life. The mid-30s and you are there. Exactly as you imagined, right?

Imagine the complexities of a broken system in which you are front line like so many of your peers. Daily struggles include always needing to be at your best every day, lest you harm your patient, get sued, or have to deal with the demons of knowing you underperformed. Patients want all of your time and all the answers (and sometimes don't want to pay for it), and you're not allowed to run behind or be late. You face an annual battle in which Medicare and other payors think you should be paid less for the same amount of work, despite inflation and most other jobs seeing even nominal annual pay increases. You hope when renewing contracts with insurers that you get a small bump for your services, but you know that you at least need to not take a pay cut. Despite living in a capitalist society you are told that you are overpaid and possibly greedy, but meanwhile, you are offering the one thing that people are desperate for and will do anything for to protect and preserve the health of themselves and their families.

Now imagine that decades later, the current version of you is very different from the teenage, high school, collegiate, even graduate school version of you. You think differently. You crave differently. Your mind is hungry for different things. Things you didn't even know about. Things you weren't prepared for. Some things did not even exist when you started this path. Some things nobody prepared you for.

Many physicians will be able to relate to at least parts of this story — my journey — because of the grind, the passion, and the determination to become a physician, to be an excellent physician — these traits exist in many of us. For many, this has been expressed through a lifelong career or pursuit. The challenges and complexities of today's medicine and those that are being faced by today's physicians are quite different from those that our parents went through as healthcare providers themselves.

Imagine one more thing. Your medical degree, your education, and your clinical experience give you the privilege and freedom to take care of patients. Consider this: your doctorate of medicine is a platform. An opportunity. A stepping stone with few equals. Well you certainly can, and most will use it primarily for practicing medicine and helping patients, but there are many other things you can do with it. You can use it as a springboard for something different if you need to. Or you can use it and your experience to supplement something else you want to do. You

*will always be uniquely positioned because of who you are, your educa-
tion, and your skill set, which includes empathy, dedication, and a desire
to help others. The world will always need people such as you.*

MARSHALL KUREMSKY M.D.

———————

SOMEONE TOLD ME MY MAJOR SHOULD BE UNIQUE SO IT GAVE ME AN
edge on getting into medical school, so I picked an uncommon
one. Molecular Genetics was offered at Ohio State and I decided to
pick that as my major, having no idea what it was even about! I
didn't consider any nonscience major as I felt it would stray me
away from the subject matter and mindset of where I needed to be.
In retrospect, it was not the right way to look at other majors, but I
am sharing this thought as perhaps a way to look at students
entering their college years and think about it in a different way.
Continuing on Molecular Genetics . . . it's a blur from there . . . but
I do remember having a really hard time learning the science
behind it. It was very granular in the genetics world and I found
the process boring. I was not a research-minded person and this
major seemed perfect for that type, not me. So "mismatch" is how I
describe the scenario at that time. I was just getting by without
killing my GPA prior to applying to medical school.

After a few waitlists and a couple of admission letters, I
attended medical school at The University of Cincinnati College of
Medicine and had a great four years. Great is a relative term for
getting through medical school, feeling crazy pressure, feeling
inadequate, and feeling like you are taking tests constantly.
Beyond that, it was still one of the better scenarios I could have
imagined. Cincinnati was a few hours from home, so I had some
distance to cover, but I still found myself going back to Columbus
a decent amount. I still had my family and close friends there and
when times are stressful, going to a place of comfort is what many

of us steer towards. On the flip side, some of the best memories of those years were making some solid friendships and getting through the challenges of school with supportive people around me. It really was a journey of bonding while navigating through a rigorous curriculum and then training with confidence for the next step. As an outlet, I did my usual workout routines (I had been lifting and running/biking since middle school and it became a part of me) and I relied on that release heavily during those years.

I was a sucker for bars and clubs and Cincinnati was a live band scene. Being single and socially hungry, I enjoyed the bars and listened to live music frequently. Looking for outlets, I found my way into a band that consisted of some medical students who performed mainly for our medical school crowd. My contribution wasn't an instrument being played, but rather singing! I had never sung publicly before. My singing was more along the lines of accompanying a great song in the car or in the shower, in other words, in a private environment. It all happened when a close friend of mine from Pathology class and I were planning an "80's theme party" and we started singing songs from that time frame. I started singing a song named "Party All the Time" by Eddie Murphy, in a high-pitched voice, and with so much enthusiasm, lol. My buddy, who was a pianist and overall music enthusiast, complimented me on my voice and said we should sing some songs while we played. That day started a whole journey of bringing a band together within my medical school class—it was one of my earliest "startups." This experience opened my eyes to the dynamics of a music band. I grew to appreciate how each artist contributed a creative element to the band, and I realized how all these strong minds made it work, or perhaps fail, as a team. This appreciation still applies to my existing world of entrepreneurship (we will visit that in a bit). That said, to this day that Eddie Murphy song is one of my favorites.

I loved going to practice and then hanging out with the band (okay, maybe goofing off). My saying I "loved" is not an exaggeration—it was so refreshing, fun, and all-encompassing, and it allowed me to escape the stressful life of being a medical student. The daily life of studying and constantly worrying about my next step was exhausting. I found that I enjoyed playing in front of a group of people—it was a release, and I just felt really alive doing it. I am definitely comfortable speaking or joking in a crowd, but singing in front of one . . . well, that was the next level. My confidence really pushed up in this new light. When we established our band and came up with some venues and dates in which to perform, we would go to our library and hang pop-up flyers for our next show, and then sit down and study. I remember the upcoming show would get me through the thick of studying—it was the one thing I looked forward to. The excitement could have taken my attention off the books and may have gotten me through this intense time without going insane . . . the verdict is still out on that. I do know that I couldn't stop thinking about which songs we would perform and how much we would party before, during, and after the show. Some people may say that they thought medical school was hard but not crazy challenging. For me, it felt very challenging and it took me to my limit of studying, staying focused, and pushing forward. During that time, I proved to myself that I could do it. And perhaps performing something new in public and getting through medical school, maybe those were the big battles that I overcame prior to graduation.

 Singing is a way of escaping. It's another world. I'm no longer on earth.

— EDITH PIAF, FRENCH SINGER AND CABARET PERFORMER

During my first couple of years of studying medicine, I was drawn to the subjects of physiology and pharmacology. I found myself interested in these subjects over most of the others—they were just more engaging to me than learning raw content. As I was exploring what fields to go into (which is really a constant exercise as a student), I discovered anesthesiology. It was introduced to me by a senior medical student who had recently chosen to pursue the field. This senior was also a teacher and student in Kung Fu. As mentioned before, I have always had an interest and dependence on physical fitness, and I started taking Kung Fu as I found it interesting, challenging, and pretty exhausting. We had a small crew that practiced in our school at certain times of the day and we all bonded over medicine, kicking, and sparring. This senior student, knowing a little more about my personality and interests, suggested that I do a rotation in anesthesiology. I learned that anesthesiology incorporated the two subjects I enjoyed deeply and that it was also considered a great specialty with regards to being a higher paying field and offering a decent lifestyle. All of these characteristics were strong enough for me to sign up for this rotation as an elective during my third year of medical school. If you notice a trend of me trying new things like singing and Kung Fu, it's that kind of knocking at different opportunities that are characteristic of me. It didn't seem like anything unusual at the time, but it was a predictor of more things to come.

In my anesthesia rotation, I had an attending anesthesiologist who took me under his wing for the two-week period and he constantly challenged me on my medical knowledge and application. At the time, being asked so many questions regarding how this worked or how I should think about it was stressful and I felt pretty dumb. It's not unusual to feel dumb as a medical student, but this scenario motivated me to learn more when I got home. It was telling that it wasn't something I was just getting through, but rather something I wanted to learn more about and be better at. My attending physician displayed a level of confidence and responsibility in running the operating rooms and gave me an aspirational sense of what a physician looked like. The motivation and excitement I felt, combined with my experience and interest in the subjects, made anesthesiology my goal. At this time I was early in my third year of medical school, and I compared anesthesiology to every other rotation. As I went through my rotations in the different departments, I kept identifying my level of personal

enthusiasm on the job to the times that I was on the anesthesiolog-
ical rotation. I really enjoyed some other rotations, such as obstet-
rics/gynecology, internal medicine, and some aspects of surgery,
but anesthesiology seemed to have the full package for me. Anesthesiology won.

Leaving medical school, the next step was getting matched.
Medical school graduates actually go through a filtering process
where they are matched up with a hospital training program . . .
and they hope for the best. As a weird, antiquated part of medicine, the concept of match day still boggles my mind. It was
similar to a day camp activity where coaches are assigned to a
group of kids and there is a teacher who picks which kids stand
here or go stand over there. It is a very stressful time where you
have proven yourself, done your best to interview, and hope for
particular jobs, but in the end, the result is out of your control and
you will be notified on a predetermined date. I wanted to match in
anesthesiology and be in a big city. I had grown up in Ohio primarily, and really craved a city life experience, so I ended up interviewing in cities that had great anesthesia programs. Some of those
included New York City, Chicago, Houston, and Philadelphia. The
process of visiting cities, interviewing, and dreaming about which
place I would potentially end up was a bit exciting, but more
nerve-wracking than desired. The matching process still blows my
mind, but perhaps on a higher level, it prepares physicians for
careers in which they will have very little control as they move
ahead.

On our big day, I was fortunate and grateful to match in the
great city of Chicago, along with some friends who also matched
there in their respective fields. I was going to be in Chicago!
Growing up, I always considered Chicago a second home. I used
to go there often to visit relatives and would even spend some
weeks there in the summers. I dreamed about living in Chicago
and even applied there for college. I applied with the hope of
moving there at that time, but it wasn't meant to be, considering
the economics of living in Chicago compared to attending college

in Columbus . . . but I was craving to be there at some point in my life. Furthermore, I was rooming with good friends from school. Having a new training job at a hospital, a new apartment downtown with friends, I didn't have any trouble integrating into city life.

With regards to training in anesthesiology at the University of Chicago, it was an incredible experience. I actually felt like the least smart kid there, and there's a good chance I was. The University of Chicago is an extremely prestigious university that many folks know about, but beyond the academic world, it doesn't seem to be as well known as some of the other prestigious institutions. I was fortunate enough to match there and eventually excel in that environment. Kudos to the quality of the students and faculty there, as they continue to impress me to this day. In addition, I will always be impressed by the renowned research and the knowledge they have generated over the years, which continues to teach many future leaders. I was skeptical of how good it really was but, damn, it really pushed me and others to be the best versions of ourselves.

After getting more comfortable with the high expectations and the high intelligence around me, I started to feel like I was fitting in and I actually started to thrive. I worked really hard. I found the work and the overall field of anesthesiology very interesting, and my motivation to learn was tangible. I became a sponge—I just knew I could learn by asking everyone around me for input and/or advice. This ability to absorb from others never really stopped, and it continues and perhaps has accelerated to this day. To reiterate this in a different way, I felt intimidated but over some time I used that discomfort as inspiration and motivation to do better for myself. I only had that one residency experience, but it opened my eyes for the first time how being at such a prestigious institution could benefit a person who was open to learning.

In addition, I also saw how being at such a prestigious institution can have a different effect on other students. Many of the medical students there seemed very intelligent, but I questioned if they were as hungry or motivated to work as hard as some others.

There are also some interactions and conversations that I recall that got planted in my memory. (After all, the journey of residency can be a bit blurry.) It's possible these students were academically brilliant, but perhaps didn't have to lean on grit as much as I had to? It was very tough to get into medical school and especially land at an institution like the University of Chicago. It was a relief to land there, but possibly that little comfort dulled the drive? Was there comfort in knowing that this place can put a stamp on your name and carry you farther than others? And did it affect your drive to do and learn everything you could? These are questions I have asked openly and the answers will probably continue to be debated amongst groups. I know that I questioned this myself a few times while progressing in my residency, but I definitely don't want to put a whole group of people into one bucket.

I loved the field of anesthesiology and at the time I was all about books and clinical work. Yes, this was completely expected, but I truly enjoyed the field and was so excited to go to the next level. In fact, when I met my wife at the end of my first year of residency, I was in such a hyper-motivated state of medical training that I couldn't imagine doing anything else. The training was intellectually stimulating, the field was known as a field for doing financially very well, and the job market was looking pretty solid —things seemed to be all lining up. In fact, I recently connected with a friend with whom I did residency training. She reminded me that I once shared during a conversation about our residency that I really liked the field of anesthesia and that I was passionate about it. She was laughing about this . . . because who really talks like that?

After my midpoint in residency, the discussion of pursuing further training vs going into practice began right away. There is a belief from the training programs that if you super-specialize in a field your job would be more secure—you are an expert at the highest level. This mindset probably isn't uncommon in the academic world where titles, tenure, and specialization are heavily weighed when measuring success. Then there is the school of thought (my school of thought!) that says we have already trained forever, there is a very healthy job market, and physicians do not appear to be getting laid off (especially when compared to almost every other field of work). Plus, there is only so much one can do to tackle the unknown or to mitigate risk—in the end, we all must make decisions that make sense first and foremost to ourselves. I realized, as a responsible anesthesiologist, that my focus should not be on perpetually training to avoid risk. I felt my training and all that I learned in four years of residency prepared me to work on my own.

Risk is always there and, at some point, you need to assess your capabilities in any situation. I think maybe that was an early sign of my "risk tolerance." When I say risk tolerance, I am refer-ring to taking risks without a guaranteed outcome. I have always seen the positive outcome or upside over the potential loss. I believe this is a trait that has allowed me to move forward more easily than others. That said, I am confident that the mindset that I utilized to explore and enjoy other business opportunities can be shared and learned, and hopefully capitalized upon by others. Discussing topics such as a willingness to embrace "risk" is the first step.

My goal was always to come back to Columbus to work. I wanted to be close to my siblings and parents, and it felt like a comfort zone. Columbus was also a great place growing up and I thought settling down in the Midwest in a mid-size city was ideal (and it was also what I only knew from experience). Also worth mentioning is that in the field of medicine going to a bigger city can not only result in a higher cost of living but also less compen-sation. In a world where you have worked your tail off for many years and incurred debt, unless there is a huge reason to stay in Chicago or any other big city, it isn't always financially the best decision. And "we" had decisions to make, my wife and I. Like myself, she was finishing her residency and was open to see how my job search went, as her field of internal medicine gave her more choices. We agreed that if I could land an anesthesia job that was a good fit, she would adapt and find a job in the same city.

When I started applying for jobs, I honestly focused on one private practice back home in Columbus—it was large, broad in scope, and had a great reputation. When I got the offer post-interview for this private practice, it was a highly exciting and emotional time for me. I still remember where I was and the feeling I had when I had a phone conversation with them. It represented the culmination of all of that studying, training, endless exam-taking . . . and then waiting for a job that paid and matched a professional income. So, even though nothing is guaranteed in life, it was a huge achievement to get to where, as a physician, I had finally ended my training and was actually able to apply it and earn a real living. I mean, it really was four years of college, four years of medical school, and four years of residency that I had gotten through. To say it felt good is an understatement.

After finishing residency, and being only one of two people who left residency to pursue a job (the other sixteen people stayed back or went to other institutions to do a fellowship for further training), I started what I called the "dream job." It was a large private hospital practice with multiple locations, which would keep my case variety high. Plus, it had a very high standard and was a reputable place that many knew about (and the partners in the practice were very welcoming). The pathway to partnership appeared to be straightforward and the financial upside seemed great, especially living in a mid-sized city with a relatively low cost of living.

As many physicians know, after residency, there is a huge learning curve when you finally start practicing independently. For me in my new practice—with new staff and surgeons and anesthesia partners—it was pretty overwhelming. There weren't any familiar faces, but it was still a much friendlier environment than where I trained, which was more of a traditional academic center with many residents in training. I was moving from a stern and impersonal environment with strong personalities to a softer space that was more focused on the patients and less on the physicians touting their own merits. It is not uncommon for academic teaching centers to have a more rigid environment in comparison to private non-teaching hospitals. Some of it may be because of the hierarchical culture of a teaching environment, which is needed to some degree, or maybe due to the fact that many of these institutions have great research going on that brings a level of pride to the physicians involved. But once training is finished, a teaching center is not for everyone. Yes, this is a generalization, but I don't think many physicians would disagree.

The learning curve with the new job, albeit stressful, was making me a better and overall well-rounded physician. It lasted a healthy few years, with my being constantly on my toes—there was never a dull moment. As an anesthesiologist, there are acute settings that require timely decisions. A "boring" day at work would be one that went smoothly and was uneventful for the most part. But, an "exciting" day at work required decisions and actions that were vital and critical. The stress level can be quite high and the patient is usually in a very serious condition on an "exciting" day. Fortunately, there weren't many days like that.

Another thing that happens during post-training is that after you take your final board examination to be an accredited anesthesiologist, you suddenly enter life without thinking about taking tests. What, wait! No tests?! This reality was constantly on my mind as I moved along to the next step climbing the medical ladder. I remember after finding out that I had passed my final board exam that I literally didn't know what to do with my free time. I would get done with work and look around like a lost dog. I had no clue what to do with myself without having a test to study for. Revisiting the journey I had had thus far, I didn't have a band to sing with, I didn't have Kung Fu with my crew (unfortunately, the Kung Fu didn't continue when in residency), and next, I didn't have any tests to take.

Then I discovered a hobby many kids and adults have been doing for years . . . reading. Yes, I started reading leisure books that had absolutely nothing to do with science or medical terms or tests —and it was glorious. Glorious is a very intentional word because, for the most part, I was done proving myself and instead found myself in a new world of discovery. In fact, all those years of my parents telling me to read didn't really sink in until I was 31 years old and had no tests to take! Either way, I got lost in some great books. A few books that were recommended and turned out to be the most interesting and engaging were *Shantaram* (St. Martin's Griffin, 2005), *A Game of Thrones* (Bantam Spectra, 1996), and the biographies of Steve Jobs (Simon & Schuster, 2011) and Elon Musk (HarperCollins, 2017).

 And the day came when the risk to remain tight in a bud was more painful than the risk it took to blossom.

— ANAÏS NIN, AMERICAN-CUBAN-FRENCH DIARIST

As time progressed working with the practice, the routine got to be truly routine—people started to get to know me, and the comfort zone increased. The desire for "boring" days didn't change, but the days actually started to get boring. After the first few years of private practice and having made a partner in my group, I was starting to get some real income that provided me with extra capital. I recall that when I was living in Chicago, I knew a few people who had invested in real estate. I was excited to hear about the opportunities, but I knew at the time that I did not have any extra capital to be able to participate (of course, I was a little bummed). My wife and I felt that we weren't in a position to invest; we didn't even have enough money to live the life we wanted for ourselves. There were so many people working their jobs and making decent money, while I was in residency on a joke of a salary, working double the hours most other people were putting in, and without adequate compensation. That said, I knew it was temporary and I knew that going into the well-paying field of medicine, I wouldn't have to feel that way much longer.

So back to real estate . . . many people around us had real estate investments and, even when growing up, I heard of and saw people buying houses, commercial properties, and even motels and hotels. When I finally started to accumulate extra capital, it was natural for me to think about real estate. I got together with even more friends and we met for drinks and started discussing various real estate opportunities. Some of my close friends were in a similar boat as mine and, like me, thought real estate could be a good first step to get into any kind of investing. With something familiar, something tangible, and—on the scale of things—something seemingly more conservative, we decided to start looking into some projects. Initially, it was a fun excuse to go out and meet with friends over some beers and discuss things other than medicine. In my mind, up until this point, we had always been working to move up to the next level (as I have made reference to with the focus on testing). As medical students, we were used to working for the next test or academic challenge. Now, in this new reality, we were facing our own challenges.

So finally learning about things other than medicine, and being able to look at investments while having money to take seriously, was very refreshing and initially quite exciting. I should mention that most of my social circle at this point were a lot of physicians. Sometimes I speak as if we were one big clan, but really I just had a lot of friends my age in the field of medicine realizing a similar mindset. So, after some discussions and plans to meet with a realtor/broker to find some deals, it all started. We met with our first broker and started looking through properties. It was quite exciting, realizing that we could actually buy as a group, and the process was pretty interesting at first. Buying as a group, or just having someone other than myself on board when doing investments or building companies, is how I have always worked best. I'm a social person that gets energized by other people and it turned out to be the team approach that was realized as we embraced the coming opportunities.

We ended up landing on a few smaller projects involving single-family homes. For a start, looking at houses that recently came on the market with the intention to rent was actually pretty exciting. I believe it was the first time I personally felt like I had some extra money to be a property owner outside of my primary residence. Touring the suburbs of Columbus and purchasing a few homes was progress, and we spent some money doing small renovations before we got tenants to sign leases. I think the headaches started when the only thing left to do was manage tenants. I don't think they caused trouble or even needed help very often, but the only time the subject of these investments came up was when there was some menial task, such as plumbing or rent, with which to deal. There were really never exciting updates on the investments or a feeling of progress. In retrospect, my initial exposure to real estate was with single-family homes and I judged this investment category based on this limited experience.

More opportunities in real estate outside of homes did come our way, but the overarching theme was that if I invested money to make money, real estate wouldn't be a bad option. But I wanted something more. I wanted something that would teach me more, something that would require me to utilize my strengths and interests in order to be productive. I wanted more than just a place in which to park money in search of returns—I wanted to be challenged and inspired. This realization started a whole new journey in my life.

A Physician Underdog Overcomes

"A medical degree is not worth anything outside of medicine."

"Outside of medicine, you are going to be looked at as an undergraduate biology major."

"You think that medicine is tough? The financial industry is much worse."

As I told my colleagues, mentors, and friends in medicine my decision to leave, I was told these concepts over and over. As I never before even considered a career outside of medicine, I wondered if this bleak picture was accurate. For physicians looking to leave medicine, I will tell you from personal experience that absolutely none of those comments are true. None.

Although I am no longer in medicine, I am now able to look back and see how the experience of going through clinical rotations years ago has helped me succeed in my financial career today. That experience gave me an opportunity to find out who I am, along with revealing my strengths and weaknesses when I was pushed to the limit. As I was deciding on my career path, I spoke with trusted mentors and friends to discuss the type of working environment that would be the best fit for me. I reached out to other physicians who had gone through a similar non-clinical career path, from a physician career coach to an attorney. I reached out to numerous individuals in the financial industry and I found brilliant mentors. All of this took resilience, open-mindedness, and a willingness to deal with rejection—I worked for it, I earned it.

As I started my financial career as an intern, I rose in the ranks as I used my medical education to analyze and discuss healthcare deals with MDs and PhDs. As I came from the culture of medicine, with little to no work-life balance, I found the financial world to be a significantly better work environment. I have built several positive business relationships, even as I practice social distancing during the pandemic we are experiencing at this writing. While this job can be challenging at times, I question whether I will ever consider retiring because I enjoy the challenges that my career brings, whether or not I have financial independence in the future.

For any physician deciding if they should or should not stay in medicine, I want to say do not make such a critical decision out of fear or lack of confidence. Whether it is a clinical or non-clinical career, make sure it is the best fit for you personally, as well as professionally. As with any industry, there are good people out there—it just takes strength and resilience to find them.

ANONYMOUS PHYSICIAN

IN RETROSPECT, I FELT THAT I WAS AT THE STARTING POINT OF MY "working career," and perhaps that inspired me to begin to look closely at other people and what their careers were like. I started speaking with people who ran their own businesses and meeting more entrepreneurs embarking on their journeys. A few things that I noticed were that these folks were focused on what was ahead of them and how they could continue to build their businesses. Decisions were made during phone call meetings or from laptops when they were on the road. But they controlled their own schedules and weren't dependent on a complex system or following rules based on regulatory law. I saw determination, I saw creative thinking converted into real decision making, and I saw the freedom that not only felt refreshing but also foreign. It was an early step at looking at my career and realizing that I was missing some pieces. The pieces had nothing to do with stability or ambition, or how to be beneficial and help people. They were about having the control and decision-making abilities needed to pave my own path. I began to feel that any future success was going to be built upon recognizing that there were pieces missing in my career and that my future was in my own hands. Becoming aware of my limitations suddenly made things crystal clear. I was in an underdog position. This thought not only continued to awaken me, but it pushed me into action on why and how to overcome that fact.

The underdog has become a big part of my character. It is the source of energy I get when learning something new, the source of energy that motivates me to problem-solve, and it has become my attitude when embracing and accepting that I am different. As a self-acknowledged and once upon a time underdog, I believe the first step to empowerment is knowing that you have less to work with from the get-go. Once I recognized and acknowledged my underdog status, I knew that I needed to seek out the tools required to turn the state around. I not only wanted to survive, I wanted to thrive. When I look back at my accomplishments and failures (we all have them), the only thing I did consistently was to move forward. I know now that it was the underdog mentality—that all or nothing, let's go mentality—that was propelling me at the time, whether I recognized it or not.

4

FINDING INSPIRATION

When I decided to pursue a career in medicine, I knew that it was going to be a long road. I knew it would take a lot of studying to maintain a high GPA in college (getting low grades isn't an option when your goal is to get accepted into medical school). For most of us, that meant we needed to take a lot of time and apply a lot of dedication and discipline to studying hard within the world of academia. It seemed like it was perhaps the only route to pursue (well, doesn't almost everyone go to college with the goal of getting the best grades possible?). If and when that lucky ticket to medical school happened, there were four more years of time, stress, and dedication to learning medicine. If we were fortunate enough to get a residency position, we then dedicated another three to seven years of training to be able to practice in the real world. The end result is that about eleven to fifteen years after high school graduation, we are physicians who possess the skills and knowledge to practice medicine. And practicing medicine is commendable, right?

But while we were dedicating our time to pursuing medicine, there were some folks helping people in other ways. This isn't an apple-to-apple comparison, but there are ways to dedicate time and energy to impact people's lives outside of the traditional vehicle of medicine. For example, take Blake Mycoskie, founder of Toms Shoes®. Mycoskie founded the shoe company in 2006 and it has become an influential brand as well as a model of social enterprise. Social enterprise can refer to when a business is changing the world for the better, or it can refer to a business using its tools to address a social need. Blake's journey began when he was traveling in Argentina in 2006 and became entrenched in the rich culture there. Along with exploring the national dance and drinking the national wine, he wore the national shoe that was made of canvas, a fabric that he found very versatile, suitable on a farm or in the city. Blake met a woman who was involved in a shoe drive, helping the many kids throughout the globe who lacked shoes, even in well-developed countries like Argentina. This encounter opened his eyes to this problem. He saw the hardships faced by children without shoes, how it complicated their lives, and even exposed them to a wide range of diseases. The experience inspired him to create a for-profit business with giving at its core. Toms donates a pair of shoes every time a pair is purchased. Over time he has given over 100 million pairs of shoes to those in need, all while creating a profitable and impactful business.

What started as a simple endeavor in 2006 by 2019 had become a company with revenues of $400 million. Toms invests a third of its profits in grassroots efforts that create change at the local level. They invest in and promote mental health, ending gun violence, and increasing access to opportunity. What Blake Mycoskie has done with his entrepreneurial path has been inspirational, influential, and definitely has helped millions of people around the world. This is an example, along with others, of what we as physicians need to step back from and examine. I want to emphasize that different pathways can lead to impactful change—some choose medicine, while others embrace entrepreneurship, corporate life, and various professional careers. I think discussing this is a start to opening up our minds to various possibilities.

Anyone can make a difference, so you don't have to
have it be some huge, global campaign, you can start
small, and that's just as important.

— BLAKE MYCOSKIE, FOUNDER OF TOMS SHOES

When we decided to go into medicine, we knew there was a
huge financial commitment involved. First is the cost of getting a
college education, followed by medical school, then continuing
onto residency, where you get paid very low wages while doing
highly skilled work after long years of training. Some of us look at
the debt we accumulated and focus on paying back the loans over
time as we settle into our jobs post-training, but I want to focus on
the lost costs. By "lost costs" I mean that as up-and-coming physicians we pay tuition upon tuition, accumulating massive debt,
while our peers have already moved on to their first paying jobs.
When we pay X amount of money into an educational institution,
we are not spending that money on investments, or courses to gain
other skills, or on travel, discovering the world around us. These
are lost opportunity costs that we don't calculate for when
deciding to invest money in one area, while also forgoing adequate
pay in order to reach the goal. This is merely an exercise to help
realize the sacrifices many of us have made when choosing the
long dedicated path to becoming a physician.

In contrast, there have been many individuals who invested
differently than those of us in medicine, and they have made positive impacts in society. I'm speaking about people who bet on
themselves and hit it big. For example, in 1990 Gary Erikson went
for a long bike ride. In fact, it was a 175-mile ride, and he packed
multiple energy bars for the trip. After eating several bars he got
tired of the taste of them and the lack of true energy they provided.
He felt he could make a bar with better ingredients and a better
taste for a more sustainable source of energy. He tried various
recipes in his mom's kitchen, using wholesome ingredients.
Initially, the bar tasted horrible, but several months later he found

47

the right recipe and named it Clif, after his father Clifford. Gary started selling these bars at bike shops around the Bay Area. The company continued to grow and, in 2000, Gary received a $120 million offer to sell. After serious thought, and a desire to have Clif Bar & Company continue to be a nutritious and socially conscious company, he decided that keeping the enterprise in his control would be the best way to preserve its impact . . . he declined the offer. After the second marriage in 2001, he and his new wife, Kit Crawford, ran it as co-CEOs, and the company continued to grow. To this day, Clif Bar & Company is still family-owned and it continues to create new product lines (including kids' bars). The company supports small and mid-size nonprofits, and they opened a certified "green" headquarters. This green categorization stems from the building complying with energy-efficient standards. All of the electricity comes from the solar array on the roof. Gary Erikson is an inspirational example of how one person can impact people and communities in a different way through purpose, time, and persistence.

 Often, for me, the best ideas come out of extreme situations in unknown terrain, whether in cycling or in business. Pushing beyond what I think I can do creates an opening for new ideas.

— GARY ERICKSON, *RAISING THE BAR: INTEGRITY AND PASSION IN LIFE AND BUSINESS: THE STORY OF CLIF BAR INC.* (NOOK BOOK, 2012)

At the beginning of our professional journey, we focused on medicine. There wasn't a ton of real estate left in our heads to explore other avenues, except for maybe just seeking some kind of an outlet. Conversations on exercise, hobbies, music or any other way to let out steam were common, but I didn't hear very many folks discussing starting other ventures or career paths. Naturally, this was because of all of the focus that was needed to be in medical school, and especially to be in residency. Yes, it requires that much concentration and energy to navigate an early medical career, but I gradually began to wonder what else we could do to help grow our interests and diversify our strengths.

I began to realize that the key was diversification. Diversify . . . I started to examine the careers of other professionals who developed their investments and businesses following a variety of paths. There are several examples of individuals who have diversified and expanded on their strengths. The best example of this, in my opinion, is Elon Musk, the cofounder of PayPal (2001), founder of Spacex (2002), CEO of Tesla (2015), cofounder of Neuralink (2016), and cofounder of the Boring Company (2016). When I have conversations about Musk and the boundaries he's pushing with his various ventures, I like to also mention that many other people have been inspired, and are building companies based on the possibilities to which he has opened their minds. Individual acts have the power to influence and impact us, whether we relate to them personally or not. My intention is not to bring Musk up to showcase him as an example of what one human is capable of doing while remaining relatable to the masses; rather than that, I want to acknowledge how a person needs different lines of thought in order to excel overall at many things. That's diversity, and it is inspiring.

 Some people don't like change, but you need to embrace change if the alternative is disaster.

— ELON MUSK, ENTREPRENEUR AND BUSINESS MAGNATE

There are also examples in our field of medicine that perhaps aren't on the top of our minds. There was a young man who, at only the age of 14, wrote and sold an article to the *New York Times* travel section. His father was a journalist and encouraged him to write. He was an English major at Harvard but had switched to anthropology when confronted with teaching standards that he felt

49

were disappointing. He felt he wasn't being graded appropriately and even submitted a George Orwell story described as his own in order to test his professor's grading process—he got a "B." I'm speaking of Michael Crichton, who went on to graduate and became a lecturer at the University of Cambridge in anthropology for a year before attending Harvard medical school. He wrote novels during this time, using the aliases John Lange and Jeffrey Hudson.

Crichton initially wrote to help pay tuition for school. In 1968 his mystery novel *A Case of Need* (World Publishing Company, 1968) won the Edgar Allan Poe Award from the Mystery Writers of America. In 1969 Michael Crichton had his first best-seller: *Andromeda Strain* (Knopf, 1969). This book brought a lot of fame to Crichton, and despite being enrolled in a prestigious medical program, he began to focus more on writing. He graduated from medical school, but the success of his novels led him to pursue a career as a full-time novelist. Crichton had many more successful titles and in 1990 he published the massively successful series *Jurassic Park* (Random House Publishing Group, 2012), which envisions the resurrection of dinosaurs utilizing genetic engineering.

Throughout his career, Crichton was criticized by the scientific community for being more of a sensationalist than a true scientist, but he was known for doing detailed research, all of which went into his work. He specifically studied the science and underlying premise of the fictional "Jurassic Park," an island theme park populated by dinosaurs created from prehistoric DNA. His diligence is something we should all take note of; in addition, we should appreciate how he utilized his research and medical background. He wrote the screenplay for the film adaptation in 1993 and its sequel, *The Lost World*. He continued his multi-media talent as he conceptualized and produced the highly successful television series *ER*, which aired from 1994 to 2009. Crichton passed away in November of 2008, carrying a legacy of being an American writer known for his thoroughly researched thrillers that often dealt with advancing technology and its ramifications.

All your life, other people will try to take your
accomplishments away from you. Don't you take it
away from yourself.

— MICHAEL CRICHTON, *THE LOST WORLD* (KNOPF, 1995)

These are examples that show what people have the capability
to do, and also how they can pursue their dreams through a
variety of pathways. It is within our nature to be curious, to
explore new opportunities, and to perhaps pursue them. Regardless of what you are doing and where you and your interests are
today, you should be open to diversifying your interests and
strengths. Perhaps this will take you on a journey that can create
long-lasting fulfillment and productivity. Pursuing a career in
medicine does require a tremendous amount of sacrifice of time
and effort in and of itself, but being aware of our intrinsic human
nature can allow us to commit to lifelong learning outside of medicine. Having multiple careers may not be for everyone, but being
open to opportunities as they appear is an exercise we should all
practice.

TOP DOGS

In 1998, brothers Ian and Shep Murray quit their corporate jobs in
Manhattan that were within 10 minutes of each other, stating that
they had been miserable at their firms. They took cash advances on
their credit cards and intended to sell ties (yes, ties) in Martha's
Vineyard. They were told it was a "dumb" idea but persisted in
starting "Vineyard Vines," a company that would sell ties. The
trend was that guys were wearing ties less often, but when they
did, they wanted to make a statement. The brothers started by
selling ties in parking lots, on the beach, out of their backpacks,
and in bars. They like to say they traded in their business suits to

instead wear bathing suits and sell ties (so they wouldn't have to wear business suits again). They sold 800 ties in the first week and started making catalogs by directly placing ties on the photo-copiers at Kinkos. They couldn't afford models so they photographed friends, which is a tradition they still follow. Their big break was in 2002 when Aflac ordered a custom tie at a quantity of 10,000. To fulfill the order they bought pizza and beer for buddies in exchange for them helping to box the merchandise. In 2004 they expanded beyond ties and in 2005 opened up their first stand-alone store on Martha's Vineyard. They still have full owner-ship of their businesses and don't want interference from any outsiders (a big reason why they launched the company). Against many odds and counter to the retail trends, Vineyard Vines is a great underdog story of two brothers leaving comfortable posi-tions in the corporate world to build their own brand, which at one point was valued at over 1 billion dollars.

 As I look back on my life, I realize that every time I thought I was being rejected from something good, I was actually being redirected to something better.

— STEVE MARABOLI, AMERICAN SCIENTIST

AS AN ENTREPRENEUR, MY OVERALL OUTLOOK IS TO ACHIEVE WHAT I visualize to be the perfect world. The first step is to consider how things could be . . . but aren't? How I would like things to be . . . but they aren't? What I would like to do at this moment, but can't? What this exercise does is take out the existing rules or obstacles that have been layered on over time, and instead focuses my thoughts on what just makes sense. For example, if you want everyone to have access to clean drinking water, then everyone should have it, right? Following that thought, clean water should be available to every community or, in fact, be available to every household. But how do we make that happen? Is it only the delivery of water that's the problem, or is it the actual supply of water that's sadly not available? I would research and revisit this exercise. Going further, let's suppose there is enough water available for drinking, but a large portion of it is used on agriculture and livestock, which for the moment aren't the problems you are trying to solve. NO. You want everyone to have access to clean drinking water. Does that mean you look at the high usage of water in different areas and try to help the situation by introducing better agricultural techniques? Do you support alternative sources of nutrition that may come up that won't utilize as much water? Does it mean that you have to come up with an economical, scalable, and sustainable infrastructure to deliver water to everyone? This is obviously a gigantic problem to solve, but the exercise itself creates opportunities on which to learn and perhaps find some solutions, all while aiming for the "perfect" world. Exploring the problems that exist and seeing what actions or inactions were done to solve them, is actually a great step to open doors for an entrepreneurial endeavor. This includes questioning the solutions that exist and then seeing if there is more to learn about or discover. This exercise will disarm the obstacles or priorities that have been placed in front of you over the years and it will help you to revisit the fundamental problems that need to be solved.

5
_____

A SHIFT IN MINDSET

As my medical career progressed, my interest in business investments gradually expanded from real estate into other areas. There
was a greater hunger, a greater motivation, and a greater interest in
looking into outside opportunities—it was empowering. I started
paying more attention to the business magazines and newspapers
that I found laying around in the different reception rooms of the
households and establishments I visited. *The Wall Street Journal*
was always in my house growing up. Early in my college years, I
started peeking into some sections. I vividly recall eating breakfast
in the morning with my dad, and he would slide a section to me
and say "See what's going on in the world." At that point, I would
be annoyed or even give an expression of true boredom, but once
in a while I would read a few articles or flip through the paper and
see what caught my eye. This wasn't that different from my mom's
technique of putting a bowl of fruit or nuts in the middle of the
table. I once again gave an expression of disapproval, but just a
little while later, the bowl was half empty or just gone. Sometimes
a great parental technique is to simply provide some things on the
table and, who knows, maybe it will be taken up and eaten more
frequently . . . or maybe not.

The more that you read, the more things you will
know. The more that you learn, the more places
you'll go.

— Dr. Seuss, American author and illustrator, *I Can Read
With My Eyes Shut!* (Random House, 1978)

So after starting my private practice job and passing my last
board exam for anesthesiology, I started to read more books, as
well as newspapers. After years of being in school, it seemed as if I
was finally able to open myself up more to the rest of the world
and pay a little more attention to what was going on around me. I
enjoyed reading the *Wall Street Journal* as it covered a lot of
different topics and seemed to touch on some global issues as well.
I found myself giving more attention to the business section. I
enjoyed reading about different companies getting attention for the
big moves they were taking, as well as the ones that were expected
to go public. Sometimes, there would be a known company—such
as Apple, Tesla, Amazon, etc.—that was said to be going public
and available on the stock market for people like me. I would read
the stories of how they started, what they went through, the challenges they faced up until their announcement of going public,
and the odds of their getting to this position.

I started relating to the products that I purchased (and the vehi-
cles that I saw on the road) to the businesses and people behind
the brands. There were people building these great companies, and
there were investors that fueled that growth. I found it intriguing
that it was in these circumstances that early investors were able to
create wealth. To the point: they were creating wealth and not just
working toward it. We are all working for income, but are we
really creating wealth that is separate from our income? Is our
money growing exponentially with a potential project or company
or real estate? We can drive our own truck, but why not have a seat
on a few other trucks that will also reach a destination and not
require our driving? Some folks would call that diversifying, or

putting capital planning into different buckets, but there is more. What I am referring to is creating wealth that surpasses any amount of hours *working* for money. And it surpasses money made through higher interest rates. It is about investing money and time early on to get a big output years later. This is a mindset and an intention for MORE. I absorbed these thoughts and considered them for a while.

 Education is the most powerful weapon that we can use to change the world.

— Nelson Mandela, former President of the South African Republic

I was intrigued by early-stage company investments. I consistently read about early investors and realized that it wasn't necessarily that they were getting a big payday, but rather that these individuals or groups had access to opportunities before the big investors got wind of them, or the deals themselves became well known. A lot of thoughts ran through my mind, such as, who are these people? How do they have the chance to say yes or no to a deal before everyone else even knows about it? And, lastly, is it possible for myself or people like me to become a part of this group of people? To me this information was crucial. I understood that, for success, one needed to know about investment opportunities early on, and—who knows!—maybe one of these startups will become one of those big companies people read about in the paper.

For younger readers, or maybe readers that are older yet younger than I am, I did not grow up in a time where there was such a thing as social media. Yes—I repeat—social media did not exist! Well, at least not in the way we know it today. When I say I would read newspapers and various books, I actually had the physical paper and book in hand when I read them. When digital books became mainstream, I did read some of the books listed in the resource section on a digital device, but my formative years were during a transitional time of technology and information access.

DURING THIS TIME OF PRIVATE PRACTICE, I RECOGNIZED THAT I HAD the ability to start saving a lot more capital—efficiently! I felt that the capital portion of investing was there ("capital" referring to the currency that I had available at that point to invest). I didn't have much experience or even interest . . . yet . . . to contribute more than that to an investment or company. My initial goal was to learn how this whole investing in companies thing worked. I kept reading about angel investing, and I kept watching the television show *Shark Tank*, which to me was helpful in that it identified how people invested and pitched. I actually give a lot of credit to the creators and producers of *Shark Tank,* along with the entrepreneurs featured on the show, for bringing interest in entrepreneurship and angel investing to the masses. It is literally like watching the American dream being pursued every week, and I applaud the show for allowing people to experience a slice of what usually happens in a private setting.

As I was meeting entrepreneurs and asking about their companies and their motivations, I realized very quickly that I was moved and inspired by hearing about the risk they took while following their passions, or just embracing the opportunities that they encountered. It was really foreign for me to take big steps

NAVIN GOYAL M.D.

forward based on a hunch or even just a feeling of purpose, especially after all of the logic and tools I had relied upon previously. It was real, and it was very inspiring to meet people going through similar motions as mine in their lives.

This is how angel investing started out for me. It was so much more than just an investment opportunity, it was a source of energy and inspiration to which I hadn't yet been exposed. I felt myself thinking about these opportunities, as well as the whole entrepreneurial world, as a place with no ceilings or rules. It was refreshing, it felt foreign, and I was excited. In addition to this new spurt of energy, I finally had the capital to invest, which was empowering in itself.

To explain further, the opportunists I spoke about earlier are referred to as angel investors. Angel investors are exactly what they sound like: people with capital willing to take an "angelic" risk on up-and-coming entrepreneurs, helping them raise the seed capital needed to start a business enterprise. The whole concept of angel investing resonated with me—there were so many potential rewards! One can get a piece of a growing company and perhaps, eventually, get a big payout, or they can just have the satisfaction of owning a piece of a company. At the time, I had no mindset to own or operate a business, but rather to invest early in a company that would allow me to have ownership without much responsibility.

There are always flashbacks reminding me that when I decided to learn the art of medicine I had picked a very challenging field and I had to work my butt off in order to achieve my goals within that arena. That said, I was a specialist in a specially trained industry, and I had put a lot of work into becoming just that. I recognized at this time that I had endless capabilities as far as learning information and skills outside of the field of medicine. I knew that I had the ability to learn, and I reminded myself of that fact whenever I second-guessed my thoughts while researching the entrepreneurial space.

It took me a while to realize the "know your value" sentiment.

Know your value. As physicians we forget that we are for the most part very intelligent, hard-working, respectful members of society, and our word—of course, combined with our physician code of ethics—means a lot more than we realize. It is important to realize that our medical degrees hold a level of credibility that allows our voices to travel much farther than those of many others. I will keep coming back to this point, but it is something that really needs to sink in. Our voice is our influence and impact, so ensuring that there are larger platforms and fewer obstacles blocking our ability to communicate, that's what I focus my attention upon.

TAKING ON A NEW ROLE

AT THE BEGINNING OF MY CAREER, ONE OF MY MENTORS WAS A HARD-working, relatively young anesthesiologist who had been at the practice for four or five years before I joined. In fact, he was a point of contact as I was interviewing for the position. He and I became close friends when I got the job offer and moved back to Columbus to start working. There weren't a ton of young folks in our group, and he was one of the guys in my age range with whom I felt I could relate.

Learning the curve of private practice was pretty overwhelming. I don't believe my voyage from residency to practicing independently was unique. All I can share is my own experience—and how stressful it was! There were multiple factors that added to the stress of starting independently, but being in a large, 1,000-bed hospital didn't help. This anesthesia practice covered 30 operating rooms and some off-site locations. When you take into consideration the staff it takes to cover all of these locations with physicians, nurses, techs, and support staff, you realize that it is going to take a long time to familiarize yourself with all of your coworkers. Even with my own anesthesia group of about 40 anesthesiologists and 40 nurses, the lack of social connection or history among them made it difficult to feel at home. In my mind, all eyes were focused on me and they were waiting for a screw-up. First impressions were and are everything, and I wasn't going to let them go to waste on my first real doctor job.

All of the new people at the hospital, and the completely new environment (I was still navigating where the preoperative area and the operating rooms were, not to mention the lounge to grab some coffee or food in between cases) was all a bit overwhelming. Add to all that, I was practicing anesthesia on my own. There wasn't anyone to comfortably call for help not only if I wanted it, but perhaps maybe just needed it (there is a difference). All of these factors contributed to a highly stressful environment and it took a healthy year, maybe even 18 months, to start getting to know people and prove myself not only to myself but also to establish myself within the community as a good anesthesiologist.

After some time getting comfortable, I found myself curious about the business of our anesthesia group and I decided to pursue positions that my partners had taken on and embrace what those responsibilities entailed. Two years into the practice I became a partner, which was the standard partner track. I was excited to be at an incredible job with great pay, a good amount of time off, and one that appeared to have a secure future. It was rewarding to be involved in the behind-the-scenes discussions, but very quickly I realized that many of the repeating issues in Human Resources (HR), and affecting the individual work ethic across the partners, weren't being addressed. In fact, over the time of my practice, I was on the board of directors repeatedly and every board election cycle, which for most positions were decided annually, felt like we were starting over at ground zero. A new president and majority of the board would reset annually and it seemed as if any progress or changes we made previously to the group or new potential business lines established were killed with new HR issues and the reset of the learning curve. I definitely felt that during my time on the board that I was more of a "sounding" board than a true influencer. I wasn't making decisions that would help us to move forward on the items that we all felt were important for growth.

In the meantime, my mentor (the one who had really up until then shown me the tracks) encouraged me to become a leader in the group. He was having some adversity with the partners and, well, it didn't end well. He was one of the hardest working partners in our group and had very high expectations for the other partners. With the spectrum of personalities and socialistic pay structure (meaning partners got paid the same, regardless of position or extra administrative duties), there were constant battles to adjust pay or just create more accountability for each partner. My mentor ended up leaving the group, which rarely happens, basically putting the medical director position of our second hospital in my hands.

I was shocked that he was leaving and very hesitant about my taking on the medical director position. The first thing that came to mind was that the hospital in which he performed the role of medical director created a lot of friction between the group. This hospital, which was in a newer and smaller location, had its own unique challenges. That said, it was not taken as seriously as our other interests because it wasn't a significant portion of revenue for the practice. It was a different workday structure and required a different pace, and changes to staffing and schedule in my group weren't tolerated well. The change and perspective that this smaller hospital introduced was less work but it created friction, the friction that basically divided our group. I was aware and anxious, knowing that by putting myself in this new position, I was automatically going to be disliked by many . . . and that was frightening.

When I think about my own personal growth, I have to attribute some of it to the major situation that occurred when I ended up taking on the medical director position left vacant by my mentor. I eventually was formally elected onto the board for two terms, lasting three years each. I started out by trying to over-communicate, attempting to bridge the gaps in communication between myself and the entire group. The goal was to take action at this second hospital. Eventually, though, I realized that my partners were separated between those that liked me and those that didn't. In other words, I had arrived. I worked hard to be in this group and my efforts to be liked *by all* had failed. I realized that this was part of growing up and, in retrospect, it was a learning process to which I shouldn't have given so much attention.

Prior to this position I wasn't comfortable with confrontation and I wasn't so confident and convicted in my thoughts to cause real friction publicly, but that was starting to change. I was a person who wanted to be liked by all, but in reality, that in itself contributed to the limiting cycle of wanting to be accepted. Not surprisingly, I survived and got closer to the people who acknowledged that I was working hard and had good intentions for the entire group. In the end, that's the key point that got me through. I knew deep down that I had the best intentions and that I was going above and beyond what was expected of someone in my position. I was able to get comfortable in this role, knowing and realizing that my intentions were good and aligned. I had a hold on the most important things: You don't have to like me and you don't have to agree with me. I know that I am putting my heart and mind into a position that helps our practice as a collective, and that is how I sleep well at night. It is also what motivates me to continue in this direction.

A Physician Underdog Overcomes

*After returning from maternity leave I was told by a faculty "mentor"
to forget having a successful career after having children. As faculty, I
was told I could not represent a project that I conceptualized, initiated,
and led because they didn't just want another "pretty face" out there. A
colleague put his hands on my pregnant abdomen and stated "Well that
wasn't supposed to happen was it?" Another informed me I spoke with
too much enthusiasm to be taken seriously . . . . Ask any woman in medicine and they could share dozens of their own stories and experiences that
parallel mine, many much worse.*

*I was raised by two loving parents, one a surgeon, who both instilled
in me a strong sense of equity and equality. I believed all people were
being treated equally, especially in the practice of medicine, where our
decisions are based on evidence, science, and facts. It was not until after
living through some of these experiences and reflecting back did I truly
realize how broken our healthcare infrastructure is for those who work
within it, and how its hierarchical structure carries with it systemic
inequities that remain pervasive even today, many years after the system
was put in place. And for women with intersectionality, these inequities
are even more significant.*

*For the last 20 years, women have made up over 45% of medical
students. In an AAMC report out in 2020, women made up over half of
the medical school enrollees. Yet, only 25% of full professors, 18% of
deans, and 18% of department chairs are female. Studies consistently
show that women's work is evaluated less favorably than that of their
male counterparts. From grant funding to performance evaluations,
awards to letters of recommendation, women are more likely to have their*

success attributed to their environment and support and are less likely to have positive adjectives used to describe their skill sets and leadership abilities.

We also know that a well-documented pay gap in medicine persists. Medscape reported that women in medicine continue to make 80 cents on the dollar compared to men, even when working the same number of hours. That can come out to 2.3 million dollars over the course of a career for a general surgeon. Even in fields where there are more women than men (such as pediatrics), where we would expect an even playing field, studies (such as Dr. Julie Silvers' research) show that women are under-represented in authorship. These disparities continue to exist when considering those working part-time, or other qualifying circumstances.

These inequities exist in medicine, but they do not need to continue. I started "Women in Medicine," a nonprofit organization, to address these issues, find solutions, and work towards closing this gap in medicine. These changes will not happen without all hands on deck, with both men and women working together to change the system. We are at a watershed moment in the world of medicine. Let's not allow the next generation of women in medicine to be bullied or harassed out of their careers. Let's fix the system and move towards a more equitable and ethical healthcare system.

Shikha Jain M.D.

The medical director role at this hospital was initially intimidating. I had never before had authority at that level. Honestly, with the respect that I had for my mentor and the other partners who were in similar leadership positions, I definitely didn't feel prepared or confident that I could handle the role. I would call this a trial by fire because my mentor left . . . but it was probably one of the best things that happened to me. We all have heard that before, right? Sometimes an event occurs that seems stressful or uncomfortable at first, but almost always the person survives, and sometimes, yes sometimes, the person thrives there.

My mentor had been in this position for several years, and he had worked hard and been ultra-responsive almost to a fault. I was walking into a staff of nurses and an administration that offered someone to call or chat with constantly, whether about staff, events at the hospital, surgeries that could be approved, and more. I was willing to work hard and represent my anesthesia group as best I could (but I was not willing to constantly keep working once I came home to the family). It took some time to build relationships within the hospital and to find a comfortable space between my colleagues and myself. That said, I eventually built a pretty good rapport with the staff. I think we all developed greater confidence in my abilities, and I found myself able to make decisions efficiently and adequately. I sensed that the staff felt I was approachable, as did fellow colleagues, and I was becoming accustomed to being in a leadership role.

Let's think about this for a second: "being accustomed to being in a leadership role?" I thought we went to medical school in order to essentially become leaders in the arena of patient care? I thought we trained in residency, while managing teams of people, whether students, fellow residents, and nurses, or other staff that was involved in patient care? When we started practicing on our own, I thought we made big decisions already affecting the lives and safety of so many people that needed our help? I thought we were asked many times a day to make decisions that people would then follow through with? That's the point! We have been leaders for a long time, we have been making crucial and life-saving decisions for a long time, but maybe it wasn't ever specifically acknowledged or titled as being in a leadership position. We are leaders and, in fact, we are experienced leaders and our actions and decisions can affect whether people live or die. We physicians must remember this, and we must bring some of that experience and confidence to other positions that are labeled "leadership." We must be okay in knowing that any leadership position entails learning new things, working with new people, and making decisions on subjects that we haven't dealt with before. Physicians need to know that they are leaders and they should think about that reality when taking on new positions.

Outside of appreciating my new role within my anesthesia group, I routinely sat in some of the hospital executive meetings. I would see many of the administrative folks whose jobs were to run the business side of the hospital. I was curious and intrigued about the work that was being done in their world before and after our meetings. I realized that many of the decisions we had to make as a group of physicians were nothing more than a formality vs our actually having a voice. On paper, it appeared that physicians were in this meeting voting, influencing, deciding . . . but I saw that much of the conversation and work had already been done *before* the meeting. It was eye-opening not only to see how the business was being run but to see how I and the other physicians were valued in those meetings. There were clinical questions and discussions in which we took a part, but when it came to the middle ground of staffing, new equipment, new programs, etc., there didn't seem to be a discussion as much as a notification of what decisions had already been made. I can't fault a business for moving in a manner by which it needs to be run, but recognizing the value of the various team members is important.

I've noticed two big mistakes regarding teams that happen during a meeting. One is to not have a diverse group of people to bring different perspectives and experiences to the table. This happens in hospitals, corporate boardrooms, and in many other enclosed meetings at big and small companies. I have come to appreciate the different perspectives that people bring that drive us to a more aligned decision. The second mistake is that while there is a diverse group of people present in the room—everyone isn't listened to or even really heard. Underutilizing the people in the room is something I see often and it is noteworthy to mention. In fact, the young or inexperienced person may be the most valuable one in the room when a purely objective observation or idea is waiting in their minds. But the environment in which they are in isn't conducive to their sharing or speaking out. Listen to them, understand them, and then utilize their input to form an aligned decision. It takes intention and experience to best use the people at the table and to get the best results.

Of course, there are many factors to how a meeting works, with regard to the hierarchy of the organization, the agenda for the meeting, and the leader running the meeting. My comfort level in these executive hospital meetings was getting higher and, in fact, I became much more confident in asking questions and even bringing the level of seriousness down a bit with some humor. I specifically remember infusing a bit of humor into a few conversations when they started getting very serious and granular on some hospital metric that I felt was trivial. I took a step back and realized that a whole group of leaders and healthcare workers were staring at a data point and thereupon thinking that the world's problems could be solved. I do believe that there is importance in going over this data, but it isn't the best use of our time and brain trust when trying to solve real problems.

This feeling came up often for me as I spent more time in different meetings and with different department heads while performing my role as a medical director. In fact, I wouldn't have experienced any of this or had these revelations if I hadn't been in the position of medical director. This role gave me a lot of confidence in my leadership abilities and in my ability to make decisions efficiently. I slowly realized that the other hospital leaders were more than peers, but rather high-level mentors. Just like in residency, I took the initial intimidation and used it for inspiration and motivation to learn more. I got to a point where my confidence in my ability to understand and engage in higher-level conversations outside of clinical matters seemed to grow. These professional experiences helped remove some of the barriers I had been facing, and I slowly began to realize that I could be anyone or anything.

The only certainty is uncertainty. And new founders and leaders are often deterred from taking risks and starting their own company out of fear of the unknown. Entrepreneurs feel they need to be experts in every aspect of their business. They consider the future of their company and have planned every step of the way as the business grows. Oftentimes, leaders make bold decisions with confidence as if they had a crystal ball. As a new leader or entrepreneur, rather than having a crystal ball and knowing the future of your company, your job as a leader should be to design the systems to allow for discovery. Planning for discovery is a powerful way to help us navigate through uncertainty and can make organizations nimble and powerful.

— SASHA SABERI, CEO OF LOUDX VENTURE STUDIO

6

OPERATION HUSTLE

At the same time that I began to realize that I was in an underdog position, I also recognized that I wasn't comfortable with that as the status quo. I hoped for things to improve and didn't accept the current state of affairs. Thinking realistically, my mind was open and my ambitions were fueled for me to do more. I wasn't going to sustain the underdog feeling forever. I had my position as a partner in my anesthesia group, and being the medical director gave me an experience beyond clinical medicine. As a medical director, I saw the ins and outs of administering a medical practice. I was learning and growing, and my new insights set me up with a background that came into practice when opportunities came calling. I write this as if one thing happened before the other, but the shift in mindset, my bold curiosity, and the opportunities that presented themselves all seemed to happen in conjunction over time. One of the first opportunities to present itself was SmileMD.

NAVIN GOYAL M.D.

Finding our SMILE

It was literally decided at the kitchen table: We were
discussing an idea and opportunity that a few dentists had
approached us with a couple of months previously. The idea was
for anesthesiologists to bring their skills and expertise directly into
dental offices. As a physician, this was a world I had never really
thought about or explored. Since the beginning of my medical
career, it had seemed that dentistry was a separate track. This was
an opportunity, and among us, there was a lot of curiosity, excitement, and a willingness to embrace the unknown. We decided that
we were going to do it. We were going to move forward.

Apparently, there was anesthesia being performed at some of
these dental practices, mostly by the dentists themselves, or by an
anesthesia-trained dentist called a "dental anesthesiologist." Less
common was a physician anesthesiologist who was familiar with
working in offices. All the physician anesthesiologists that I knew
were practicing in hospitals, surgery centers, or part of practices
that serviced operating rooms and obstetrical units. The biggest
eye-opener in this was the fact that anesthesia was being done in
office locations and we, as physicians, didn't know very much
about it. I found this motivating, and with my two close friends,
who were also anesthesiologists, we were ready to dig in and learn
more about the field of office-based anesthesia and about the
opportunities it offers.

My two partners, Ajay Satyapriya and Tarun Bhalla were more
than just friends. They were like brothers. I had known them since
grade school in Columbus, Ohio. At the time, the Indian community was small and we bumped into each other frequently at some
of the events to which our parents took us. Our parents were
immigrants from India and they found culture and comfort in
spending time with other Indians who, like themselves, had come
to the U.S. in search of greater opportunities. As children, we had
the benefit of mingling with other first-generation Indian-Ameri-

cans. Our parents were all immigrants who had made the move and assimilated themselves and their families into a new country. Our friendships were unique to our life experiences, and many relationships were built among our interactions. After playing tennis, having sleepovers, becoming extremely close friends (even after high school), we developed the common goal of going into medicine. It wasn't uncommon for an Indian-American to want to pursue that career path, or to have had some healthy pressure or guidance from our parents to go into medicine. It was something that the three of us had in common—our heritage and our parents. As a result, we worked hard, got incredible parental support and guidance, and made it into medical school. Although we were extremely close friends, we ended up enjoying and appreciating the field of anesthesiology on our own accord and we three independently applied for our residencies.

The fact that all three of us ended up in Chicago for residency was an incredible gift. We had our hard-working years, but also plenty of fun experiencing the great city that still holds my heart. I met my wife in Chicago. She is also a physician in the field of internal medicine (to this day she is still passionate about medicine and helping people via the hospital practice for which she works). My wife, Mili, and I worked hard during residency and got married soon after meeting each other. We were both grateful for our career opportunities and were motivated to work hard and learn as much as we could in our respective training. I remember that our lives were so busy during these years that we forgot our first month's wedding anniversary. It doesn't seem like that big a deal in retrospect, but it highlights how busy we were and how much time and energy was sacrificed to get through it all.

A few years later, we moved to Columbus and settled into private practice jobs. As mentioned before, I would call my job there my dream job. It was an anesthesia practice that was well known in the community. It had a wide variety of cases in hospitals and ambulatory centers, a high standard of physicians that came from different training programs, and the healthcare system that was contracted with the group were extremely reputable. It was literally everything that I had worked so hard for, along with a great compensation structure. Being in medicine was and always will be an honor, and I worked hard to achieve that position. What I hadn't yet realized was that there was a part of me that wanted to do more, and really could do more.

As I speak about my evolution—being at this practice and gaining other interests—when the opportunity (which became SmileMD) came along, the idea of working with my two closest friends laid a solid foundation. It's really hard to find trust and comfort in any relationship, but to have that in my life while pursuing this endeavor was a huge advantage, which I believe led to its success. I think it is important to give some history to the co-founders with whom I moved forward on what may be a revolutionary company.

As an anesthesiologist, there were tons of thoughts swirling around in my mind, including how to get medications, insurance, supplies, and having backup plans and processes. We were excited about this opportunity and we didn't want to take it lightly. My partners and I all had full-time anesthesia jobs, but these other endeavors sounded different and they were exciting to consider. A section of our minds and a part of our ambitions that weren't before utilized were now being . . . and there was no feeling like it. We were fortunate to have had each other, and we constantly called or texted to discuss the A's to Z's. I attribute a lot of our ability to move forward on this opportunity to have each other to trust, to encourage, and to mitigate some risk by avoiding a solo endeavor. I do credit a lot of my success as an entrepreneur to team building, finding colleagues with whom I can work, and who could fill in gaps that I saw as missing. I also value having work partners whose ambitions are closely aligned with mine. This is a consistent piece in my journey thus far.

We moved forward, we opened up some accounts, came up with the name SmileMD, and then tried to figure out how to start a business. None of us can recall how the name SmileMD came about, but we wanted something that felt dentistry facing but also incorporated MD. It's an important step that we can't recall, but we have been happy with the name. The core of the company was anesthesia, which the three of us knew as experts in the field of medicine, but we were taking it outside of a controlled environment and building a business—uncharted territory! It was scary, it was exciting, and it was fun to continuously think about "what next" would take us out of our comfort zone. This to me is everything about entrepreneurship: It utilizes different parts of your brain to problem solve and ultimately helps you discover comfort in the uncomfortable.

 Starting a company was not easy. It took hard work and a bit of luck. It's a bit like walking. The first few steps are unsteady and it's so much easier to go back to crawling, but if you stick with it, it will become something you can't live without.

— Ajay Satyapriya M.D., Cofounder SmileMD

When we got our first client, I still remember the three of us screaming in the car as we left the dental practice. I'm talking about screaming with joy in making a "sale" from a business we created from scratch. We had presented our story, how serious we were taking the business for safety and service, and how our process was going to help the practice flow smoothly. This practice was a very reputable and busy one, and we knew there was a large opportunity there and at other practices. The practice had said they wanted to try us out and that if it went well and they saw value, they could give us more business and be a referral source. It was coming together. We still had a lot of work to do, but as entrepreneurs, we needed an opportunity, and this was an early one in which to prove ourselves. We did some cases at this practice and as a result, we learned a ton. I still remember discussing it that day with Tarun and Ajay, my partners in SmileMD, when the cases started. When it was finished, we downloaded details on what more we should consider and try to improve when moving forward. It was a lot of work modifying every aspect of our care and of our business. As three individual anesthesiologists with different backgrounds can come up with different scenarios that can go right, or maybe go wrong, we felt that we had the core medical knowledge to build the anesthesia delivery aspect. With regard to building the business side, we had a lot of work ahead of us.

I started to reach out to people in the Columbus startup community who were looking for help growing a business. I ended up in a circle of folks that included my old friend Darshan Vyas (who I will mention more about in upcoming chapters). There was a lot of startup activity going on in Columbus around 2015, and I became a huge fan of the energy, creativity, passion, and hope entangled in the world of entrepreneurship. I made many acquaintances from whom I received help and direction. What I also observed was that I was not alone in my endeavor to get help. There were new and experienced "founders" within the start-up business community, and they were all looking for business development, networking, funding, and help just getting it all done. (This observation will come into the conversation later as I discuss the founding of LOUD Capital.)

As we were building the company, networking for clients, and getting providers, we realized that there was a lot of work to be done that we three founders did not have enough time to do ourselves. We hired a practice manager from the dental world, which provided us with a full-time person to find business and answer calls. We weren't making enough money to afford a practice manager's salary, but we realized we needed to invest more capital into the company and staff it appropriately to make things happen. There were a lot of discussions and, frankly, some disagreements on what we should do. I think it's worth saying that disagreeing isn't the big deal here and that, in fact, I feel it's extremely important and healthy to listen to different thoughts and perspectives. I do think realizing this and being able to move forward with a common goal is what helps a team get through the frequent decisions that are molding the company that we were trying to build.

 Entrepreneurship is pure hustle. It's about operationalizing a game-changing idea. There are 'lightbulb' moments that make you feel invincible, and hurdles that make you feel minuscule. But the journey is worth it!

— TARUN BHALLA M.D., COFOUNDER SMILEMD

The decision to invest more money into the business is what I feel changed the trajectory of how the company grew. Could we organically build a business that would eventually make a profit? Would we be able to build a great customer service experience? The answer was yes . . . But then, didn't we want this company to be so much more? We discussed that expanding our services was a goal of the business and, in order to really give it a shot, we needed to invest in people and processes to make it big. We were willing to shut this company down and lose some money if it didn't work, but that burden was small in comparison to learning and guiding the business to its full potential. Personally, that is a strength and a weakness of mine. If I believe in something enough or see what something could be, I will take a risk more frequently or farther along than perhaps many others would. It can obviously take one a few steps forward or a few steps back, but that's the thing: if you sit on your ass, you aren't moving. Again, I know it can be a strength or a weakness.

After we saw progress in the company with a new manager and learned a lot more about the distinction between the medical and dental world, our team gained the positive reinforcement needed to continue investing in the business. We learned that the dental practices and dental industry itself not only had their own culture and ways of doing things, but they didn't want people from the medical world trying to change what seemed to be working for them. They were open to improving and learning new ways of doing things, but coming in as physicians and touting how we could improve safety significantly, as well as improve efficiency, didn't seem like the best approach to building trust. These subtle yet important nuances opened our eyes to how others could bring their experience to *our company* and affect our mindset and approach.

We continued to bring in more folks as we learned the gaps we had in the company and the pieces of the puzzle we didn't even know we were lacking. When it came to us founders, our practice manager, and the physicians who would perform the anesthesia for the cases, we felt we needed to find someone to help streamline the accounting, utilize technology to help us be more efficient, and bring a higher level of business experience to further guide us. We were approached by a colleague who I had met in downtown Columbus at the accelerator, and he was starting his own consulting business. Ryan Retcher, who had a background in banking and most recently guiding startups through an accelerator program, knew about us and SmileMD, and had an interest in working with us to solidify the business, in which he saw a lot of potential. He pointed out things we should have been thinking about and how he could help fill those gaps. Once again, it was more money out of our pockets, but Ryan seemed like a solid guy and, in understanding his recent experience, we recognized that he was willing to do the job very economically for several hours a week in an effort to help start his own consulting business (while helping us where we needed it most).

Ryan played a large role in transitioning us to the next phase of the company: at that point, we three founders had to get comfortable with having two people helping the business while we were at our day jobs. To really emphasize the scenario at the time, I was a full-time partner at my anesthesia practice, which included taking overnight calls and covering some weekends. I had two young kids and a wife who was working part-time with her hospital job. The extra time we had after all those responsibilities went to the side business that now required more time and attention. And my co-founders were in the same scenario with full-time anesthesia jobs and raising young families. It wasn't an easy or ideal scenario, but we had started something that made us eager to pursue this journey. In fact, maybe it was not a time burden but an outlet of creativity and excitement. The company was growing and there were some large opportunities ahead of us. Eventually, the discussion of what the company could be, and the full-time attention and resources required to bring it to the next level, came up more frequently in conversations. What could the company become if we had someone running it full-time vs part-time? It was a discussion that led us to think about how big this company could be and what elements were currently missing in our business strategy that could take us a step further. What else could we do to grow this business . . .

Less than two years after starting SmileMD in 2014, we brought on a CEO to run the company full time with the intention to build and scale the business. My recommendation was an old friend from Ohio State, Saket Agrawal. Saket was already situated in a comfortable leadership position with a large company in San Francisco. We connected while I was visiting California, and over a few beers and conversations, we began to speak about starting to run a business and other entrepreneurial opportunities. (Never underestimate a conversation about the future over a few beers. It can change the trajectory of your life.) Saket shared how he had gained insights and learned so much over the years in his diverse experiences as an engineer, an MBA, and managing a large team in the technology industry. At this stage, he wanted ownership of his choices and his potential. It was timely that we were having that beer. While Saket was once a schoolmate, we knew each other primarily from social events and common friends. One thing I knew of him and his whole family was that they were intelligent and had credibility within the community.

As Saket and I were talking about what SmileMD was at that point and what it could be, I saw that his mind was turning. He started asking a lot of questions that clearly originated from a fresh set of eyes. The more we spoke and the more we engaged, I saw what could be. My original intention wasn't to ask him to join the company, yet our conversation ended with my saying, "Hey, you should run this company!" That statement planted a seed and over the next few months, we continued to speak on it. He flew home for the holidays and we continued the discussion, landing at a high consideration. We knew we were small in size but big in vision. As founders, there would be sacrifices on our end in finding a way to compensate him, but there were also huge sacrifices on Saket's side leaving a stable and well-paying job. He made his decision. He left the comfort and stability of a great tech company in San Francisco and joined SmileMD as the CEO. (As I share my journey in writing this book, and tell of the risks I personally took to pursue a greater opportunity or calling, you will see that I am not the only one taking this leap of faith. Relating to anyone pursuing similar paths to yours makes it more real, more possible, and perhaps more motivating.)

 The glamorous part of entrepreneurship is the vision of how you want to fundamentally change the world. What keeps you going day in and day out is a drive to make that vision a reality. The part that is mentally and physically challenging is the million steps of piecing it together because it's only you and the people you convince to take on this Herculean task who are trying to make it happen. People sign up thinking it's for them then realize it isn't sexy. It's crazy.

— SAKET AGRAWAL, CEO OF OFFOR HEALTH

By bringing on a CEO, we were investing our own capital into the company to ensure that it could grow to its full potential. Our next step was discussing the goal of raising capital in order to go beyond our home city of Columbus and scale the business nationwide. We knew we were helping patients and practices in a new way, and we knew that help was needed beyond our geographical area. Thus, in 2018, we raised a seed round to get capital in the business to help invest in more staff and operations in exchange for equity to the investors. Equity, or stock in our company, was sold to investors (angel investors) who believed in our company and wanted to invest. Now, we had new investors and some fresh capital to continue to grow the business, which is what we did. In fact, we began to expand our business into other cities, and many physicians and practices became customers as well as proponents of safely enabled in-office procedures. For the record, many startups fail. It takes much more than capital and a great idea. It takes a sound business model, smart financial management, a talented team, and a clear goal of what the company should be doing with respect to its goals. To raise capital past a seed round is an achievement in itself.

 Tradition becomes our security, and when the mind is secure it is in decay.

— JIDDU KRISHNAMURTI, PHILOSOPHER, SPEAKER, AND WRITER

When we entered two other states and the number of patients who needed us increased, we were propelled to hire some talented executives, along with investing funds into technology that could support this new patient load. We were able to raise a Series A funding round from a few venture capital firms, which was a huge milestone for the company. Series A is a round of financing (followed by Series B and C) by which a company is able to grow by selling equity or shares. Series A financing can be a great step for a startup in need of capital and, when raised, it is a validation for investors that there is a strong enough business model and strategy for the business to grow into a money-making enterprise. The investors are mainly venture capital firms or family offices.

We utilized our Series A money to continue hiring highly talented people, invest in technology that enables us to grow into more states, and work on other service offerings. It was a very proud moment as statistically to get past startup obstacles and to receive Series A funding, we were already placed in a small percentage category. Many of us know that most startups fail, and to get past that phase and to successfully receive a Series A is note-worthy and a validation of the hard work that had been put into the project thus far.

THE BOTTOM LINE

THE SPECTRUM OF RAISING MONEY FROM SEED CAPITAL AND THEN ALL the way from Series A to B to C, and so on, until eventually being acquired or having the option to sell your stake in the company, is what is needed to grow and expand a business. There are different ways to finance and move through different rounds and they are necessary when trying to raise capital. The first official and vali-dated round of capital comes from firms or family offices, and it is referred to as a Series A round of funding.

There have been a lot of ups and downs since we started, but the moral of the story is that we moved forward on our journey and we took risks at multiple points in order to explore and enable our potential. In my opinion, there wasn't any specific talent or unique passion or excitement that brought this all about. My part-ners and I just chose to move forward on a unique opportunity. We simply did it. At this writing, it has been seven years since the inception of SmileMD, and although it is still our main line of busi-ness, it has become a part of a larger vision called OFFOR Health, which will connect patients and healthcare professionals in local communities. We are currently seeing patients in three states and have been having discussions with many other states in an effort to serve their healthcare needs. At this writing, we employ and are responsible for over sixty employees, and have taken care of thousands of patients. From a few guys in a kitchen discussing an opportunity, we now have an impactful healthcare company that is influencing how health care is delivered and has created jobs in different markets. Not a traditional use of a medical degree right? I don't think tradition really belongs in this book anyway. On to the next . . . .

7

LET'S GET LOUD

After co-founding SmileMD, I started reaching out to folks in the Columbus community and I met a lot of great entrepreneurs who were doing big things. I was exposed to startups exploring pathways that included education technology, healthcare technology, wireless power applications, and even hydrogen energy, to name a few. There were so many great people in my own backyard who had intentions to build impactful companies, and the one underlying theme I learned from all of them was that it was difficult to find funding.

I had been in touch with my old friend, Darshan Vyas, who was actively helping companies grow and figure out pathways to success in the entrepreneurial space. Darshan and I had gone to Ohio State together, but outside of social events, we didn't know each other all that well. That said, I knew he was always involved in some business venture and definitely seemed to be excited about entrepreneurship. When I was in medical school, Darshan worked for a brief stint at a commercial bank. He quickly realized that in corporate life—a work environment with too many rules and regulations, and without people around you who listen to your ideas of innovation and creativity—he wasn't going to last. He quickly decided that this wasn't his idea of working or spending time wisely. He left that job to pursue his own business ventures and made a good living in the medical transcription space.

Darshan had been angel investing for a few years and had had many startups that never took off. As he was gaining entrepreneurial experience, he realized the founders needed more than money to launch a successful business. They needed trusted people around them for business guidance, as well as solid business plans and strategies. They also needed to have the ability to understand the difficult journey that they were embarking upon as entrepreneurs. There are plenty of people who get passionate about entrepreneurship and start something. But the key to success is not just to want it, but to want it *so much* that you succeed, and when you hit the inevitable obstacles you just don't stop. Every obstacle is yet another challenge that must be navigated . . . and overcoming each one as it comes is how you reach your goals. After Darshan realized that investing capital into startups wasn't enough, he decided to provide help to emerging businesses in a more structured fashion.

Darshan got together with some people who appeared to have similar goals to start an accelerator (this included Ryan Retcher from the SmileMD story). The term accelerator refers to an individual or group of investors who provide services specific to startups. Emerging businesses refer to an accelerator early on their voyage, seeking to be guided in some fundamentals of business models. They are given clarity on their goals and visions, receive a foundation of branding and marketing, and are simultaneously plugged in with mentors—mentors being crucial components to bringing experienced folks in, who in exchange get a small equity stake in the business. The goal was to have these entrepreneurs learn a lot from other entrepreneurs and mentors. They would fulfill some of the foundational objectives of the accelerator in order to be prepared to receive some seed capital. As a reminder, seed capital is the first money invested in a company to begin developing a business or product.

Darshan and some of the other people I had been speaking with agreed to raise capital from investors to fund these companies when they went through the accelerator. But running the accelerator with a focus on building and guiding these early businesses was the priority, and fundraising went onto the backburner. That said, raising funds is a necessity for accelerators to help their entrepreneurs continue to move forward and achieve their goals. Raising capital is not the same business, nor the same approach, as running an accelerator. Raising capital can be tough and it requires an intentional effort to communicate to investors how this capital can be used to increase value. The credibility of the people raising capital is always in question. In the end, investing in a fund or a company is a testament to the credibility and capability of the team managing it. I will come back to raising capital for a fund shortly.

Darshan and I were discussing SmileMD and how his accelerator (or at the least, his experience and network) could help grow our business and connect us with other folks who could be helpful. As we got to know each other on the business side, we quickly realized that we were aligned in such a way that we saw entrepreneurship as limitless, and that we equally cared for people and how we treated them. We also quickly agreed that embracing collaboration and working in teams was the best way to grow productively, and meanwhile offered more fun to the founders and investors by giving us the ability to contribute and work as a group. Together, we were approachable and reasonable people. Those characteristics seem simple and perhaps trivial, but they are a large part of how our story continued.

As I got more excited and involved in this accelerator, and the energy and people involved, I became an advisor. This was an informal position, but through it I learned how the accelerator worked and what some of the challenges were that we were facing. Darshan was an energetic and upbeat person, yet recently seemed very frustrated. He was expressing how some of the companies were finishing the accelerator phase but there wasn't enough capital raised yet to invest in them as promised. He felt these companies were investment-worthy and it would be disappointing for them to have put in all this time and effort and then not receive the capital that would enable them to launch their product or business. Being an angel investor and meeting some visionary entrepreneurs, I invested my own capital in some of these companies. I felt these were great entrepreneurs with more structure and promise than many other startup companies. I also appreciated the fact that these entrepreneurs had become friends and colleagues with some of the people working at the accelerator, as well as with some of the mentors and advisors who had been helping them on their journey. Since many entrepreneurs don't have that community and mentorship around them, some of the early risks of investing in a startup were mitigated by these friendships. This belief in community and mentorship to help fledgling entrepreneurs is fundamental in my approach to business, and I will always hold this value close to my heart. Community and mentorship make the journey more meaningful and fulfilling for founders and investors. They help start-up companies overcome the obstacles they face as they set out on their journeys while making the entire experience more fun and impactful for everyone involved.

Back at the practice, I wasn't quiet about the things we were doing with SmileMD and being plugged in with Darshan at the accelerator. I was very excited and I was constantly talking about how different and engaging I found the world of entrepreneurship. There were plenty of stressful days and times juggling my anesthesia job, growing SmileMD, and advising startups, but it was my time to spend and my choice to be in that position. A sense of liberation and a feeling of being inspired were the two forces that kept me driving straight from my medical practice to plugging into the startup ecosystem. As I continued to talk about this experience while at work, some of my medical partners and other coworkers at the hospital became intrigued. They were curious and asked many questions: How did you start your journey with SmileMD? Who are these entrepreneurs with whom you have been spending time? And, there were many questions of simply, how? They had the interest but they didn't have the know-how. Many of these physicians had a desire similar to mine to expand from the medical field and invest in start-up companies or just explore outside opportunities in general. I slowly became a source for these new partners regarding information on deal flow and investment opportunities.

I want to take this opportunity to share how all of this really went down. Meaning, how did I pull time out of the practice in order to pursue multiple ventures? Did I have any special circumstances or extra time allotted to me? All while I continued to be present and aware at the anesthesia practice and SmileMD. Even further, I was a conscientious husband and father. In the end, I did two things that I feel were crucial to not only building the companies and pathways that we were working on, but they also presented the most productive and fulfilling experiences to help us achieve our goals. In fact, at this point, I was so passionate and excited about entrepreneurship that instead of spending my free time watching television or golfing for several hours, I would network and connect with people who could keep me moving forward on my entrepreneurial endeavors. In a corporate meeting with my anesthesia practice, when I was being questioned how I had time to start SmileMD, I told one colleague that instead of going to a bar or hitting golf balls for several hours, I would go downtown and meet with entrepreneurs and try to advise various companies when I could. This is a starkly different mentality from that of many other people, but my outlet was entrepreneurship. I liked going to bars, socializing and had a respect for golf, but we choose what we do with our time. (Many of my anesthesia colleagues were avid golfers so it was pertinent to most discussions.)

The other crucial component is that I trust and rely on others to be team members. I can only do so much as one person, and I rely on other co-founders and colleagues to help drive what I helped to start. While I was working in the hospital, there were other people continuing our entrepreneurial work with the belief that we were building something of value. As a collective, we were motivated in the goals that we were pursuing. It's important to emphasize that the many hands and minds involved continued to build and move our interests forward, even if I wasn't physically present. In conclusion, any free time I had was intentional, and the opportunities to share what I was building was always my preference over doing things solo. I truly believe that this mindset has multiplied my time and multiplied my impact to this day.

With the issues that Darshan was facing at his accelerator, and with my confidence and familiarity growing in the entrepreneurial world, we decided that it would be a great opportunity for both of us to open up a small angel fund. An angel fund is a structure where investors put capital into a common private fund, which is then used to invest in start-up companies in exchange for equity. Angel investors usually give support to start-ups at their earliest stages, the time when most experienced investors and/or firms need to see more validation and traction before considering backing the enterprise. Angel fund managers help run the fund and determine the companies in which to invest. We reached out to an attorney in the community and received guidance as far as the next steps needed to cover legalities and documentation. With legal steps taken, and a deal flow in front of us, there was increased interest and confidence in ourselves as investors, and we started having conversations about our entrepreneurial endeavors with some of my physician friends at work and within my circle.

Deal flow is a term used by finance professionals—such as venture capitalists, angel investors, private equity investors, and investment bankers—to refer to the rate at which they receive business proposals and investment offers. Being in a burgeoning startup ecosystem in Columbus, Ohio, and getting to know the entrepreneurs currently engaged with the accelerator, there was a good amount of deal flow in front of us. From an investor standpoint, there was a lot of interest and excitement to participate in projects like ours. I was energized and soon enough we created a fund structure in which we planned to raise money to invest in some of the companies that we felt were great opportunities.

When I speak about fund structure, I'm referring to the investment strategy and business model that investors put capital into. Once the money is raised, how and where is the capital invested? How are the managers going to perform the diligence? And, how are the investors and managers going to make money on this capital? Specifically for our venture funds, the strategy was to invest in early-stage companies that were run by people who were ambitious, hardworking, and trying to solve real-world problems. The problems being solved needed to have a business model around them that would not only make money but would sustain the business itself and continue to solve the problems at hand. It's not a simple task trying to validate or confirm that the business model will work, but these were the conversations that I was pursuing.

Many of these conversations were part of our diligence, finding gaps in which we could help as strategic investors. We used a 2/20 model, which means that when capital is raised, there is a 2% annual management fee. When money is made from companies exiting or being sold or acquired, the principle that the investors put in is returned, and then, moving forward, the management takes 20% of the profits and the investor makes 80%. This 2/20 structure is pretty standard in the venture capital world and we went by that structure.

I have mentioned strategic investors and I have mentioned the value of community and mentorship in regard to the success or failure of startups. Next, what Darshan and I thought was common sense and good business practice was to get to know the founding team, figure out the challenges of the next several steps in their company's journey, and utilize our own network to help the company overcome those obstacles. We talked about how hard it was to find funding (which is why we started the fund). We agreed that it is important to continuously help the founders, and eventually to become a sounding board for them as they set out on their journey. We recognized that our being there to give guidance and support would eventually help the company win, which in turn would help us and our investors win. We heard stories of many investors and firms becoming silent partners; the funding came in but expectations weren't met as far as the utilization of the investor's expertise and network in helping the portfolio company. The big difference between us and others in the industry is that we were entrepreneurs, and having that mindset and experience helped shape how we operated as investors. We were engaged, and we were empathetic and willing to help our new founders. We wanted to have open communication with them as they pursued their goals. We were ready to move forward with our time and money to help our founders' businesses thrive and grow, but we had no intention to be silent.

LOUD CAPITAL

THE NAME LOUD CAPITAL WAS CREATED FOR OUR COMPANY AND IT was specifically attuned to our philosophy of being loud and active investors and not silent investors like others in some of the stories we had heard. We agreed that we would raise capital from investors and be the best stewards and the best fund managers we could be. Our intention was to be approachable, bringing our network and experience to the table. We would likewise be trustworthy and respectful when doing business. We were passionate about entrepreneurship. We knew that the more we helped these start-ups, the better they would do and in turn, we, as investors, would do.

Traditionally there has been a misconception that venture capital is only limited to a select few wealthy individuals or families. Our mission is to make venture capital resources more accessible to the people.

— DARSHAN VYAS, COFOUNDER AND CHIEF GROWTH OFFICER AT
LOUD CAPITAL

The mantra of win-win became our philosophy. In fact, we actually talk about the triple win in this context because the investors, the founders, and anyone in the company, including the employees, and the people who benefit from the company's services and/or products, are all winners. Yes, people. Regular people. When we were looking for companies that had special traits, or differentiators that made them stand out, I didn't realize that we were doing things differently. Our philosophy of investing was consistent with how we wanted to build ourselves as a company. My version of entrepreneurship was about people. My goal was to find how we could help each other in the pursuit of success and satisfaction in whatever pathway or vehicle that we chose. This may seem like a common-sense statement, but in the world of venture capital and investing, there can be many person-alities and backgrounds that get focused on the financial rewards with blinders on, and they forget that there are people right in front of them. With Darshan's and my goal of trying to be reason-able and approachable, with both of us being entrepreneurs, all these things added up as differentiators and they are what made LOUD Capital impactful, accessible, and why it has resonated with people as a purpose-driven brand.

So we had a good amount of deal flow and a great philos-ophy that we felt would help the founders and our companies get started. Next, we needed to focus on one of the most chal-lenging parts of starting a fund from scratch: fundraising. When it comes to fundraising . . . well, that is a whole other animal.

The first thing I tell people is that fundraising isn't for everyone. It can be very stressful and arduous, and you have to be determined. As the investors can be individuals, groups, corporations, or institutions there is a varied spectrum of what is expected of you and your team when fundraising. They are investing in you and the management team, the credibility of the surrounding team, and the strategy of the fund. You have to build upon the confidence that their money will be in trusted hands with the potential to make a profit. Profit isn't guaranteed, but all those aspects are discussed when investors are approached. Fundraising can take time and effort to educate, inspire, and create the excitement that is needed for a successful partnership. I am also speaking from the fact that Darshan and I had no previous fundraising or venture capital experience. We realized throughout our journey that what we were accomplishing was pretty incredible, but it was far from straightforward. Welcome to entrepreneurship!

The capital for this initial angel fund was raised pretty quickly and many of the investments were made into companies in which we had done diligence. In the early stage of researching and vetting an investment, diligence explores the opportunity and the potential market for the vision. That said, I quickly learned that it was even more important to learn about the founder or team of founders that were driving the vision. It was important to get to know these people in order to assess their moldability for the upcoming journey of entrepreneurship and to find out their reason for pursuing this journey. I use the word moldability to express one's willingness to listen to others, to consider other options or pathways when different from your own, and to understand that this needs to be a constant exercise. Making decisions, changes, and learning from other people and their experiences are the crucial traits a business venture needs in order to succeed. The reason for pursuing the journey in the first place should also be heavily weighed. It is important to ascertain the company's motives, because when times get tough—not if, but when—you need to know how committed they will be to overcome those obstacles vs letting them truly stop their endeavors.

When we committed capital to some of these companies, the founders expressed much gratitude for our believing in them and their vision. It occurred to me that while we were feeling fortunate to have had the opportunity to invest early in these companies, the founders in return felt even more excited and validated by the investment. It's not easy raising money for a company. They expressed how tough it had been to raise any capital and that our check, averaging $25k–100k at the time, was a boost for the company, as well as a positive reinforcement of the journey on which they had begun.

There was a lot of work ahead because beyond raising capital, utilizing that capital in the most productive way for the company was a huge challenge. There isn't a rule book or a road map to figure all these things out. This is where strategic investors and mentors can really help guide a company on a path that they can follow in order to move forward. There is nothing simple about it. Perhaps it is the challenge that makes the whole world of entrepreneurship so meaningful and engaging to me. It's a challenge, and it affects people in unique ways. There aren't any rules to follow. We are faced with obstacles on a daily basis. It is very different from problem-solving in a known context. It's problem-solving in a changing environment, with different people, various levels of challenge, and evolving expectations. But differences are what often keep us engaged and excited. I never imagined what was ahead. Can you imagine how empowered my partners and I felt as entrepreneurs who had just started a fund? This wasn't expected, but it is where we were. We were pursuing an opportunity and then found ourselves in a whole new world of meaning and impact.

After a few successful investments the word got out pretty quickly in the entrepreneurial world and the requests for meetings and funding started to come in. As I have mentioned, it's very hard to get funding for a startup, so any source of capital is precious, especially in the Midwest, where venture capital and individual funds are not as plentiful as in other parts of the country. As entrepreneurs reached out to us, we had even more potential investors asking us for our insight, investment thesis, and ability to get deals. And there was a new curiosity generated by the people who were already in our network. My physician colleagues started asking more questions, and the level of interest amplified once we opened and closed our first angel fund.

The number of investors grew along with the number of business opportunities in which we could invest. We even had the opportunity to enable companies to go from conception to start-up. Yes, we suddenly opened up a windfall of everything entrepreneurship. To put this in perspective, it was 2015 in Ohio, where there was a very young venture capital ecosystem compared to the coasts. That said, there was an opportunity to shape the ecosystem and do it the way we felt made sense. Think about that. We entered a space that was an open field of opportunity and we spent a lot of effort educating ourselves on angel investing, investing time for equity, investing into growth companies, and facilitating investors into deals, as a few examples. This was a huge undertaking and as I write this, it's kind of crazy to think about. We really didn't know what we were building and we didn't know how much the entrepreneurial ecosystem needed our work. But what started out as a simple endeavor between two guys became a company with a large mission and a great group of people supporting it.

 We were two guys and a fund, but I guess that's how anything really starts. Small and simple with the intent to keep moving . . . and who knows what can happen.

— NAVIN GOYAL M.D.

A LOT OF INDIVIDUALS DON'T HAVE A DEEP KNOWLEDGE OF THE entrepreneurial world, so we started by spending a lot of time sharing our vision, outlook, and goals in an effort to educate others. This became a big part of who we were and what we did as a team. We were educating others on what we had learned on our journey. We weren't experts or experienced founders with a long history, but we were curious, working hard, and our intentions were good. We wanted to make money, but we also wanted the company to be impactful. To clarify, we were pursuing a meaningful endeavor that would likewise be meaningful to others. I believe that having a career as a physician, where the environment is about how we are trained to help people and not focus on personal financial gain, had a lot of influence as I stepped into the business world. In fact, I see plenty of discussion and action to make personal financial gain in the business world, but I don't see or hear enough about how our investments can help other people. I believe the two spectrums, helping people and creating a personal financial gain, are at the heart of a business that is impactful to yourself and to others. This is the only lens through which I have viewed and experienced entrepreneurship, and I really embrace this perspective whenever I see an opportunity to drive purpose and profit. Pursuing a purpose and being intentional about building a good business model around that purpose, can be a profitable endeavor. That is a deep belief that I hold and it helps guide my decision-making, not unlike the Hippocratic Oath.

We wanted it to be an exciting investment for our network as well as one for the other investors with whom we had been working. Win-win right? The impactful description above also applies to entrepreneurs in this space. I don't see it any other way. There are different ways to make money in the investment world, and the way I see it, along with my team, the goal is to make all sides happy. Considering the time and effort needed to move forward on a venture, one that is beneficial to us as well as to society as a whole—we all win, we all feel good about it, and the work really does reflect our intentions. We speak about our actions and the opportunities to bring impact to our investors who may not be involved in the day-to-day, but they know that their capital is driving purpose and profit. It's a cycle and if you have the opportunity to experience it, there is no turning back. The people who are watching and learning by your example have already become intrigued, inspired, and perhaps are ready to jump into the cycle.

We continued to get new investors, open new funds, and expand our offerings beyond venture capital. People who weren't particularly interested in venture capital, or wanted a variety of opportunities with different levels of risk, were the ones to whom we strove to educate and offer deals. We became a much broader firm, sourcing and curating private investments and introducing opportunities that would engage many types of investors. We expanded the team, we expanded into other markets (the great cities of Chicago, IL, and Raleigh, NC), and we started to become a real brand. LOUD Capital is an alternative investment firm that educates people on the private markets and introduces ways to invest, with the end goal of creating returns for investors while supporting the overall community.

 What I am most proud of about and for LOUD is our passion for bringing education and opportunity to as many people as possible. With this mindset, we strive to share our experience and resources with current and potential investors, to show them ways to expand not only their mindset but also their financial knowledge and portfolio.

— Marshall Kuremsky M.D., Partner at LOUD Capital

GLOBAL IMPACT

DURING THE EARLY STAGES OF LOUD CAPITAL, DARSHAN AND I WERE
focused on expanding the business and meeting with many
different people. We had a friend who represented clients in China,
and he was intrigued by the venture model we were building. His
name was Ethan Huang, and by that time he had already been a
McKinsey & Company consultant, business owner, and, more
recently, a consultant for Chinese investors. As Ethan got to know
us and learned about our passion for starting LOUD Capital, we
started spending more time together, brainstorming on what
international opportunities there could be for our team. Ethan felt
our entrepreneurial way of investing would be of interest to some
of his clients, as many of them had already invested in real estate
and businesses in the U.S. Even though this was much different
from real estate, he felt his clients could benefit from these other
investment opportunities. As we started discussing what value our
portfolio companies could bring to some of these foreign investors,
we spent a lot of time and effort trying to understand what
investors would need in order to make informed decisions. We put
a lot of effort into exploring, building, and developing a deep relationship with Ethan, which bore fruit for us years later.

After about a year of navigating different opportunities with
Ethan, he moved to China to fulfill some personal and business
obligations. He moved to the fast-growing and progressive city of
Shenzhen. For those who haven't visited this city before, it has a
population of about 12 million, a beautiful skyline of relatively
new buildings, and it is known as a global technology hub. Ethan
moved there with the intent of working on building his client base
and continuing to expand services to his existing clients. He
learned pretty quickly that venture capital, business building, and
entrepreneurship were topics that many in China wanted to learn
and hear more about. Ethan started having conversations in
various circles that led him to larger audiences and, eventually,

placed him in front of some government officials. He shared the LOUD story and the opportunities that we were working on in the U.S. Ethan, being a well-spoken and intelligent individual who can communicate about large opportunities, found himself to be in a circle of policymakers and industry professionals that were aggressively shaping the future of China. This was where and when a real opportunity presented itself.

Between many phone conferences and trust among friends and colleagues, we set forth planning a trip to China. As our energy and opportunities gained steam, Ethan continued to navigate the potential of doing business on behalf of LOUD Capital. Our whole LOUD Capital team was flying into Beijing to meet with some government officials along with private business owners who hoped to further explore these pathways. We wanted to continue to build relationships and expand on what Ethan had been working, so we decided to ask him to work with us on building a global network. There were entrepreneurial needs and opportunities in the gigantic ecosystem of China, and although we knew it would take a lot of time and effort in a very different cultural and political system, far away, we took this risk knowing that the outcome could be large and impactful.

 Great minds must be ready to not only take opportunities but to make them. I believe that is the true interpretation of the underdog mentality—an empowering force that drives one to create resources and solutions out of the limitation and, eventually, reaches the self-defined destination seemingly impossible by all measurements.

— ETHAN HUANG, PRESIDENT OF LOUD GLOBAL IMPACT.

The first China trip was eye-opening, to say the least. The architecture, the design of the cities, and the overall cleanliness of the environment were all a revelation. My partners and I honestly had expectations of a colder-looking, more mundane skyline, but we discovered, and then learned, that there was a diversity of design, and their fine arts were the result of multiple collaborations between nations. We met some of the young entrepreneurs who dreamed in the manner that we did; they were excited about various technologies and hoped to eventually build their own businesses. We had conversations with different government organizations expressing our intent to pursue a more global business. We discussed the current political tensions and how they shouldn't inhibit either side from helping solve problems. Political tensions shouldn't prevent problem-solvers from solving problems, and they shouldn't put the country's needs and goals on hold. We felt that as a company visiting from the U.S., it meant a lot for the people in these organizations to see how serious we were. Their recognition of our sincerity and passion allowed us to start building trust. They expressed how they wanted to work with more people from the U.S. and hoped there would be more American visitors. We learned the long-term visions of the Chinese entrepreneurs with whom we had met and how they wanted people, resources, and companies to grow in their country and were seeking for us to be a part of that strategy. All in all, it was an eye-opening experience and it was extremely motivating to be in a position of leadership. In fact, it really felt like we were a larger company than we were, and that made me realize that it's all perspective. In the U.S. we felt like a startup trying to prove ourselves to everyone around us, but heading into China with the groundwork that had been laid, we felt like a large company that could choose its own path. This was a very rewarding experience that gave us a peek into what our future could look like. We left China with a burst of motivation and excitement and had many more conversations exploring the next steps to follow in our new business partnerships.

Being a physician lent me the credibility needed to navigate the high-level conversations in which I was engaged. It provided me with my purpose of entrepreneurship and impact and opened my eyes to how a physician's background brought a high level of respect to conversations. It's probably worth mentioning that with the traditional cultures of India and China, and their having large populations, the pursuit of becoming a physician is extremely challenging in these areas with a high number of applicants and limited spots. It's like that in many parts of the world, but the sheer population of these countries tends to push it to another level of scarcity. Culturally, in these countries, there is a deep respect for the medical field and the physicians there who are seen as "healers." There is a high level of appreciation for the sheer achievement of someone becoming a physician. There is another level of credibility when it comes to your becoming a physician in the U.S.; it is looked upon as a coveted spot in which there are more resources and elite training. Thus, having medical training in the U.S. garnered a high level of respect in communities around the world, even within the physician community itself. This realization led us to ideas that perhaps we hadn't automatically considered, yet they were there as we opened doors and pursued our paths.

In the next two years, we had some of our Chinese partners visit the U.S., and we were able to have them meet with various corporations and businesses relevant to our discussions. We took them to four different cities and continued to dig deeper into forming a global business strategically . . . and together. While we were experiencing our trip to China, and realizing the needs and opportunities presented there, our Chinese partners came to a similar conclusion after visiting us here. Both teams recognized that we could build a stronger foundation by working together and as a team, doing business in what we hoped would be an effective and efficient manner. We went to China later that year and continued to build more partnerships and explore more opportunities that existed there, especially in regard to entrepreneurship and education.

Today, this global strategy and foundation have become known as LOUD Global Impact. At the time of this writing, our headquarters reside in Beijing with the intention of bringing companies from China over here to the U.S., and vice versa (a two-way street). This allows these overseas companies the opportunity to grow in this country, and meanwhile, get exposure in the Chinese market (the attraction being that they had a plan and structure in place). Building this relationship has taken a long time, but we are confident it will be impactful to many people and businesses. We are proud to have built a brand new pathway that can be used as a roadmap for other countries. If I were to present an analogy of how I see different countries doing business, I have a vision of a path created by a few stones in a stream that reaches from one side to the other. It's possible to get over the stream and onto the other side, but you must go one at a time, and you must be careful, there isn't a guarantee that on the next day the stones won't be covered deep in a body of water. The stone path also doesn't encourage people to cross, as there are too many unknowns. We took a long time to build a bridge over the stream. It took risk, a lot of people, and a lot of effort to connect both sides, and it took the belief that people wanted to cross from one side to the other. In the least, it took the fact that people who wanted to cross had a foundation to do so, and we anticipated that the word would spread and bring the two sides together.

THE VENTURE CAPITAL SECRET

THERE IS SOMETHING WE FOUND IN THE WORLD OF VENTURE CAPITAL that I've started to talk about in conversations, and want to continue to speak about on a larger scale so more people can learn about it. There are some questions, such as:

Do you know how powerful venture capital can be?

Do you know a lot about how venture capital firms pick their companies or founders?

Do you know what happens when capital goes into a founder/team and what that does to the people or community around them?

Do you know that the interest in venture capital is very high and there are a lot of people who want to learn how to run a fund or be part of a venture capital firm?

THERE IS A GOOD CHANCE THAT YOU DON'T KNOW THE ANSWERS TO these questions or have even asked yourself any of them. I spend time dwelling on these questions and hold myself, my team, and all of my stakeholders accountable for the responsibility I feel within the industry of venture capital.

There are two different sides to any investment opportunity: there are the investors (the venture capitalists) and the investees (in this case, the company's founders). With the investment, the investees gain an advantage that creates many more opportunities for them as they move forward to raise capital from other firms. The presence of investors can enable a company to hire more people and grow the company in various ways. It can even bring these companies additional tools by which they could get more clients or customers, which can snowball into a business growth cycle. At the same time, the founders (investors) now had an advantage in the eyes of the entrepreneurial world. Their investments, as venture capitalists (VCs), put a seal of approval on these start-up companies. Investors knew that these companies had passed due diligence and that they had provided validation to interested companies that their enterprises were investment-worthy. In return, the interested companies provided investors the confidence that the company would provide a good return. In the end, the initial steps by the founders were a huge step forward for both them and the company.

When investors make the decision to invest, there is something deeper that occurs outside of the capital. A foundation of empowerment is built, as the founders have an edge now over others that didn't get investment. This comes back to how powerful venture capitalists can be, because they have the ability, through their endeavors, to empower these companies. In the spectrum of changing the trajectory of the company and everything it touches, the venture capitalists are in a position of power and it was not one that was appointed, but rather one earned through raising money and then being in a position to invest (as seen fit). Most potential investors don't know that this power exists, and as my experience got deeper in the industry, I was presented with opportunities to educate. After companies realized their newfound position, the next step was asking some important questions: How do we seek out our deals and how did the founders get connected with us? Did the founders have a common friend, possibly one of our venture partners or associates? We also have to ask questions to ensure that we are educating ourselves and others on how to invest in these opportunities. Do men and women ask or apply for funding in the same manner when representing their company? Do people among different cultures ask or apply for funding in the same manner as others when representing their companies? Do people among different communities apply for company funding in the same manner? Do all the different people above-mentioned have friends and family with similar connections and wealth? The quick answer to all these questions is NO! Further, are these questions being asked within the closed doors of venture capital firms across the world? I would bet that they are not and that many people and communities have invested in these endeavors without realizing the truth. There are powerful decisions being made, without investor oversight or input. Decisions, such as which companies to invest in as venture capitalists (VCs), are currently being made dependent upon the result of conversations made behind closed doors. And these decisions are extremely important, not only for the success of the investors but for everyone who has committed to the endeavor.

Outside of the ability of the founders to give a start-up company some edge, they offered them the opportunity to help raise more capital and grow the enterprise. The investment empowered many young people and adults from the community who were watching with curiosity and were inspired to maybe one day follow in our footsteps. These people will become our future role models and people of influence. In the eyes of the venture ecosystem, these start-up companies were validated by receiving our investment. Think about the influence and insight being offered to the people, on both sides of the table, who were watching and hearing about the opportunities being pursued. It's powerful. It's very powerful.

 Our industry is still too insular, too old, too risk-averse, too white, and boring . . . We are here to unfuck it and make sure that venture funding opportunities are equally available to everybody.

— Timothy Wolf Starr, CEO of Atlas Venture Partners

Where am I getting with all of these statements and observations? What is the purpose of pointing out the power of venture capital and investment firms in general? As I have learned about this industry and seen what impact we can make as investors, I have come to recognize that we have a large responsibility. We must ask all of the questions above, with the intention to invest responsibly with inclusivity, accountability, and transparency. In this way, our processes can constantly be improved. The manner by which I am looking at this space may seem ambitious, but the more I uncover and understand how people can differ within communities, and have different experiences and results when seeking investment capital, the more I want to discuss. I want to get my investment peers in the venture capital space to not only listen but to start asking questions regarding how we can improve this industry and provide more impact as a collective. There is a lot of money and time already being spent with minimal to no impact on society. In fact, I believe that if more investment firms participated in this thesis of investing, more problems would be solved and the world would be a better place. I'm telling you, this is very powerful and influential stuff. It shapes people's jobs, their families, their communities, their earning potential, innovation, education, and so much more.

For the record, I am one person with a small team but a big vision. I am also the one writing this book, but the book is about a very special team of unique individuals that have helped me along this entrepreneurial journey. I wanted to make sure that it's understood that it was teamwork that carried LOUD to where it exists today. That being said, I am dedicating my time and energy to speaking, writing, and acting on this big vision. It's possible that I saw and experienced the power of entrepreneurship and investing early in my journey. It's also possible that my medical degree gave me a foundation to think about people in a different light. I do know that I am utilizing my medical degree in a much broader way and bringing that ethical code to the field of venture capital and entrepreneurship. For those not experienced in the field of medicine, I took the Hippocratic Oath when I was in medical school to "First do no harm." This oath was very important to me and to my colleagues when we were making decisions and had huge responsibilities when approaching each and every patient. It was a helpful guideline when thinking about treatment, how to approach a situation, or just how to communicate with a patient. I think "first do no harm" is a very impactful message that can help guide people in all walks of life.

When I came into the business world, I saw a huge spectrum of ethics and am still shocked at how there aren't any standards similar to those of physicians, the Hippocratic Oath. Why must one pursuing any professional career not have some guidelines and/or rules to follow? Currently, I don't have patients in the medical field, as I am fully in the VC/entrepreneurial world, but I do have a lot of people in my sphere with whom I have the ability to educate and empower. I am bringing the Hippocratic Oath into the field of venture capital and entrepreneurship in an effort to impact the world on a different but equally important scale. This thought process and responsibility are behind the mission and tagline for LOUD Capital as Venture For People®.

VENTURE FOR PEOPLE

1. The belief that venture capital can create a positive impact in society.
2. A pursuit of investing in diverse and underserved communities.
3. The responsibility to educate and inspire the next generation of entrepreneurs to embrace this belief.

I HAD TO LEAVE

WITH ALL THE MINDSET CHANGES, THE REALIZATION OF MY POTENTIAL as a physician and entrepreneur, and the increasing frustration at my anesthesia practice, I had to go. Had to? Ok, maybe I was so frustrated with my existing job and frustrated at not being able to give my full self to LOUD Capital. What I had to do was make a decision for myself. Yes . . . I had to make a decision that would save *me*. It wasn't healthy juggling all of the things that I was. It wasn't fair to my family to be so tied up and preoccupied all of the time, but I wasn't in a financial position to just get up and leave my current position. I had a family to support and I had invested time and work into achieving this great anesthesia practice and position in order to meet my goals. I have never been irresponsible when making large decisions and I wasn't going to start, but . . . this was my pivot point and it *had* to happen. The old me perhaps would have been content, or at least would have figured out a few outlets to stay grounded while working at the anesthesia practice —a job that most people would consider a dream, especially in the field of medicine—but this wasn't the old me.

> It was really hard for me to understand why Navin was leaving his job. Anesthesiology is such a desirable field in medicine and I felt he had such a fulfilling and secure job as well as a great work/life balance. I was stressed too because we were such a young family and I didn't know how stable this new field would be. I now strongly feel he did the right thing—he saw an opportunity and found a way to share his ideas and move forward. I'm so proud of how he has used his education and medical experience in this new direction.
>
> — Mili Goyal M.D.

When I flew back from my first trip to China, I was overwhelmed by how exciting the week had been, how I felt to be in a great leadership position with the team, and the realization of how I felt very comfortable and confident in continuing this journey . . . I got very emotional. Actually, I'll admit I cried a lot on the plane ride back, realizing how special and grateful it felt to have this opportunity as an entrepreneur. Crying isn't something that occurs regularly in my life. In retrospect, I feel it was the transition that I was going through and the flood of new emotions that was overwhelming and, to be frank, special.

I acknowledge now that I didn't miss my medical job and that I needed to work toward leaving it. I am sharing with you the diary entry I wrote on the plane back from China on November 17, 2018 (it's a diary entry so pardon the horrible grammar).

 > What a trip!! I mean it was the best week of my life so far. Business on a whole new level. Impact. Nice people and intentions, plus our team is just so solid we walk in as a comprehensive team. China is great. My mind and my eyes are much more open. The global things that we will be doing now. . . It was so much fun—I think I had more adrenaline surges and amazing moments than I ever had in such a short period. I wonder why the media intentionally doesn't mention a lot of positives in China and in other countries. The only way to find out is to go and see it for ourselves. I really hope we can turn momentum into action and *I can leave the hospital job soon.*
>
> — NAVIN GOYAL M.D.

The highs kept coming in the next couple of years, not in increased frequency, but enough to really know that what we were doing was fulfilling, exciting, and just felt more real than any other journey I had embarked upon. I wasn't getting any highs from my hospital job. In fact, I was experiencing some lows on difficult cases and/or days, and I was in a neutral zone most of the time while performing anesthesia. This isn't unusual in a medical job, or perhaps many jobs, but I wasn't able to get any highs and I felt that in itself was very telling. After planning financially, seeing the opportunities in front of me, and knowing that I had the backup to practice medicine if I needed to, I made the decision in July of 2019 to send a letter to my board stating that I was going to leave my partnership at the practice and my last day would be December 31st, 2019. I am including some of the content I wrote to the board of directors on July 29, 2019.

Fellow Board members:

*I wanted to give you a heads up on my recent personal pathway.
As most of you know I've been on an entrepreneurial journey for
the past five to six years. Obviously, I co-founded SmileMD and
shortly after that, I co-founded LOUD Capital. I have realized
that entrepreneurship is very challenging but very rewarding for
building something from scratch. That being said, LOUD Capital
has been my interest for the past four years and I've been working
hard to get it growing.*

*We have opened up an office in Chicago, Beijing, and we have our
HQ here in the Arena District. I say that because we are
expanding and my time needed to continue the growth and the
exciting things that we are doing are required more than ever.*

*As great as this job is, and the people who comprise this organiza-
tion, my mindset has changed over the past few years by receiving
personal fulfillment outside of this medical career. Obviously, it
wasn't planned nor initially desired, but here I am in a position to
impact a lot of lives in a very different way.*

Navin Goyal M.D.

If I were to tell you that I sent this email, which was sitting in
my draft box for weeks, from a train in France . . . would you
believe me? I was actually sitting next to one of my daughters on a
train from Paris to Bordeaux, soaking up the beauty around me
and really enjoying the laid-back culture. It occurred to me with
clarity that I was definitely going to leave my practice, and that I
needed to let my board know soon. I will never forget the liberation I felt just by pushing send, followed by a few texts to my close
friends, letting them know it was really happening . . . the rest of
the vacation in France was just that much better.

And then there is the most dangerous risk of all—the risk of spending your life not doing what you want on the bet you can buy yourself the freedom to do it later.

— RANDY KOSIMAR, CO-FOUNDER OF CLARIS, FORMER CEO OF LUCAS ARTS ENTERTAINMENT, CHIEF FINANCIAL OFFICER OF GO CORP, AND "VIRTUAL CEO" OF TIVO

8
———

THE EMPOWERED PHYSICIAN

I have come to the point where I reflect on this untraditional journey and ask questions that may help other physicians who are going into medicine, or actually anyone who wants the field of medicine to be the best that it can be. What would you change in your journey? Would you still become a physician? Do you think physicians could be doing more?

 Most people will choose unhappiness over uncertainty.

— TIMOTHY FERRISS, ENTREPRENEUR, INVESTOR, AUTHOR, AND
LIFESTYLE GURU

I understand that my story, my experience, is not a roadmap for most physicians, but there are realizations and things that I have learned along the way that I want to share. Sharing my journey was a huge first step in understanding how a shift in mindset and intention can occur, and my goal became to empower physicians, or at least help them to lead more fulfilling lives. I believe my insights offer physicians more control over their destinies, and perhaps can help some of them leverage their moral compass in a manner that impacts the world in a positive way. At the core, I will always be a physician by training, with an ethical mindset to spend my energy on helping people. But now I am thinking about how this energy can help in a broader way. I am an empowered physician and my goal is to empower my physician colleagues.

There are a few traits that I feel physicians should have in order for them to make real change for themselves and to further their impact on others. I have utilized these traits to further myself into a very unique position, and I am extremely empowered as I continue to utilize them and share my insights with others. These traits include, but are not limited to, having an awareness, moving forward, taking risks, knowing your value . . . and opening yourself up to new possibilities.

When discussing the underdog, I have mentioned having the ability to recognize that you are in that position. If you recognize that you are in an underdog position, it sets up a different game plan for what to leverage in your strengths. It encourages you to pay attention to how you and others can shift weaknesses and keep them from getting you down. In other words, there is value in realizing your state and the state of physicians currently. Recognize that this awareness is the first step. The next step is learning how to leverage the capabilities that we do have as physicians, and begin the journey to overcoming the underdog position. My call to action for the physician underdogs who are ready to move forward:

Develop an Awareness

Awareness is something that I didn't have early in my medical career. I'm specifically speaking about the awareness of what is going on around us, while we—physicians—are focused on working in our field. This awareness includes recognizing that decisions are being made to shape the healthcare industry, while we—physicians—are seeing actual patients. The awareness that decisions are being made to shape our careers, while we—physicians—are working in the field. And the awareness that we aren't part of the conversation in a truly effective way . . . again, while we —physicians—are dedicated to our work caring for our patients and community.

The first thing to understand is that the world is being shaped, influenced, and impacted by people who may not have the same intentions and / or moral compasses as those of a group of physicians. Being aware of this, physicians are now prompted to think through the possibility of infusing our ethical code and intent in such a manner that we can help people beyond traditional practice. Perhaps we can broaden and shift—as individuals and as a group—to find more profound and meaningful ways to reach and support people. Yes, we take care of patients and have the medical space of our expertise, but should we be influencing people in ways outside of healthcare? Being aware is a wake-up call. I'm determined to bring awareness to physicians who don't have the luxury of stepping outside of their day jobs.

Speaking to physicians (and perhaps everyone), this awareness will help shape the world as you view it. Your intent to help people is great but your current impact potential is much more limited than you think. My goal is to make physicians aware of these limitations and stress the need for amplification of personal intent outside of a structure *that wasn't made by you or for you*. It is the only system we—as physicians—know, but I have first-hand experience that currently physicians are only aware of a slice of life. Right now, physicians exist within a small and controlled environment, which does not reflect the full truth of what can be.

The awareness I have been speaking about will help you when you feel like you don't have control over your time, your finances, or even your mindset. This awareness will help you understand the certain lack of respect you perceive when working within the system. This awareness may make you a bit uncomfortable, but I believe it is what is needed for REAL change to happen. You need to increase your awareness, you need to stir with discomfort, and then be intelligent enough and ambitious enough to make change for yourself . . . and perhaps contribute to society in a whole new way.

> Every human has four endowments; self-awareness, conscience, independent will and creative imagination. These give us the ultimate human freedom. The power to choose, to respond, to change.
>
> — STEPHEN COVEY, AMERICAN EDUCATOR

My awareness began to expand when I was in the position of medical director for a community hospital within a large medical system. I was observing the dialogue and the agenda in front of me and realized that there were many meetings, and discussions prior to the meetings, all in which I was not included. I got the impression that I was there as a figurehead—a physician who, as a fellow team member, put his blessing on the agenda items. There wasn't anything specifically that bothered me upon that insight . . . other than realizing that there were full-time teams working on policy, strategy, and management, all while we physicians were seeing actual patients. What I said at the meeting really didn't matter (unless it was something alarming), but the awareness I gained at that time woke me up to the people and efforts behind the scenes. These people had a significant impact on what was happening, all without any input from physicians. I'm actually not questioning whether a hospital and/or a medical system should be run by nonphysicians. What I am speaking about is an awareness that when we physicians want a change to happen or want to influence how patients are taken care of, we are set up to be very limited in our input. That was an awareness. And that is the awareness of which I am speaking.

I was part of a large anesthesiology group and sat on the board for several years. Outside of HR and some routine business discussions, we would constantly play defense with our hospital contracts and demands. These weren't strategy meetings seeking to expand or a typical call to action for business growth, instead, they were more to the effect of "let's try to preserve and keep what we have because it seems like a pretty good deal ." I am not picking on my board or even on my group and the system in which it was a part. Rather, it was eye-opening to think how many physicians and physician groups were thinking that way: We are only as worthy as the best "deal" out there. We have been working in a system that we have little control over, and even though we were a private business, the tone of the conversations was not as expansive as those of a business should be. Attending these meetings brought an awareness that we, as physicians, didn't have much control over how money was spent in the hospital and what the priorities were there. The decisions on what supplies and equipment were needed, where we spent time, and even the cost savings of being efficient and safe didn't carry over to our group. It sounds more like an employee position versus that of a decision-maker. And we had to accept what was given to us.

A social post that I recently saw is an example of how my current awareness has helped me see things a little more objectively. There was a celebratory post of how vascular surgeons were keeping their reimbursements the same, as there was a threat of getting some of their reimbursements cut. I was shocked to see the joy when all that was happening was that they weren't getting a pay cut for something that they had earned a long time ago. It was even more obvious when I mentioned this to a non-healthcare friend, and his response was "so you're telling me the people who save lives by preventing people from bleeding out are just trying to keep their reimbursement the same?" You have people who are getting COLA (cost of living adjustments) and overall getting some increases in pay over time for their performance, while we physicians are used to spending energy on not getting punished. This is where awareness comes in and can help physicians get out of the underdog position. So what do our minds demand and how can we nurture them in order to be the best version of ourselves? The goal is to bring an energized level of attention and detail to medicine, while not depending on medicine alone. *Awareness can help us participate in the change that is needed.*

 One key personal leadership lesson I've come to practice is never to form an opinion of anyone. How they are at this moment is all that matters. How they are tomorrow, I'll come to experience over time, as 'tomorrow' still needs to be created and nothing is concrete.

— Nishad Parmar, Senior Partner and Chief Investment Officer at LOUD Capital

Intend to Move Forward

There was a point when I realized that every person doing big or small things decided to focus and go down a certain path. I remembered that becoming a physician was a huge endeavor that demanded hard work and dedication. I knew that if I wanted to broaden my horizons or put myself in a better position, I had the ability to do it. I had the intention to not stay in my up until now frustrating career of only medicine and become a person who could be in a leadership role, who could be in the boardroom of a company, who could be a person on television speaking about a specific subject matter . . . . I felt empowered and imagined myself being in these situations. I asked myself, why shouldn't I be there? The intention took my available time and turned it into a drive to meet people and learn as much as I could. The intention gave me permission to do what was necessary to grow, to move forward, and to put myself out there.

One of the lessons I have learned over the years is that the difference between people who move forward in life vs the people who seem to be in more stagnant states is that the movers have intention. Intention is a word that I hear more often in the media and in conversations about yoga, spirituality, entrepreneurship, purpose—just about anything that is worthy of talking about. It's obvious to me now that when people start having conversations about their intentions, it's actually the start of a plan to move forward. Why, over the years, do some people move forward while others seem not to progress on their journeys?

Moving forward is something that I hear about a lot. Just do something. Just take a step. Just make it happen. All this translates into taking what's in your head and converting it into something actionable. It is really that simple. But there is a psychological block that many folks submit to that puts them in a *could have, would have, should have* category. If you look at the steps I have taken and where I am today, it is clear that I am in my current situation because of my actions. These actions led to more opportunities, which then presented even more actions to take, some of which wound up offering me completely new paths to explore. While the initial steps that I had taken led me to a completely different position, mindset, and even career, it was the fact that when opportunities arose, I recognized when to take action. I haven't spoken a lot about this, but at the time my own thoughts were questioning me, "what am I really getting into?" and there were people in my circle asking themselves the same question. For every step I took, there were many around me that spoke about action, dreamed about action, and even questioned me about why I chose to take or not take action. Those people may be content with their scenarios right now, but I believe most of them are in the same place as they were when I last saw them. In the end, everyone has a choice. Taking action and moving forward is the game-changer.

I believe this whole book explains the many steps I took to move forward, and I hope there are examples you read where I tried something out, and something came out of it, whether that was an opportunity to grow as an entrepreneur or as an individual.

You should be that individual, the one who feels like they have control.

You shouldn't let that obstacle stop you, or prevent you from being a better version of yourself.

You shouldn't let anything or anyone prevent you from realizing that you have that choice.

You should be the one who moves forward and asks people on the sidelines to come with you.

Be Willing to Take Risks

So we began with awareness: The knowledge that the field of medicine demands attention and detail but does not address our lives as humans. We are human, and we have personal needs such as time, self-care, good mental health, good physical health, creative outlets, and much more. This is just to say that medicine and all of its good and bad can inhibit us from experiencing other needs in our lives. The next step to empowerment is the intention to move forward, to start expanding your mindset, to start thinking bigger, and explore what else is out there. After that, you need to have the willingness and ability to take risks.

When it comes to taking risks many physicians first react with an emotion or feeling of defense. Physicians are traditionally risk-averse . . . or perhaps being deep in the field of medicine has made us more risk-averse. It's not crazy to say that a field so rich in science and research encourages a more evidence-based approach vs a direction that is unknown and may have risks. Either way, it's a topic that I want to discuss, and one that I think is necessary for the broader perspective that is required for physicians to make real change for themselves and others working in the field. When I say risk, it can be pursuing an entrepreneurial endeavor, or maybe just investing time and/or money into something unfamiliar. By embracing risk, I mean essentially going into a mode of discomfort or into an unknown journey that pushes you to learn about something new.

When I was admitted into medical school, I specifically remember feeling celebratory and embracing the accomplishment after all of the years I had spent getting to that moment. I also remember thinking that I was now set for life, or that I at least had the opportunity to be so. The current state of physicians may entail some comfort or even dependence on this sense of security and stability. Because of that, many physicians rely on the field and devote all of their time and attention to it. Now, I still feel that working hard for security and stability is great and commendable, but it should come with some caution. Striving for security and stability is what most of us want, but the end result is a sense of comfort and ambivalence, where the drive to learn more, do more, and feel more becomes a lower priority. This, in turn, can lead to a lower sense of fulfillment and a lack of purpose. When there is burnout, a lack of fulfillment, or a feeling of not being in control, there has to be a real change in a physician's mindset in order for them to reach a different, more fulfilling place in life . . . and the only way to get to that greater destination is by taking risks.

As I have said, risk can be learning about something unfamiliar. Perhaps you want to learn about business and how to apply what you have learned to your practice and/or your personal finances. Maybe you just want to be knowledgeable about the business side or the logistics side of how your medical system is run. What steps would you take to get started? There isn't a right or wrong answer here. That said, I've heard so many responses to the effect of "Well, I don't really know anything about business, so I usually just ask my financial advisor or a friend who runs a business." Does this sound like the trait of a physician who is a proven learner, ambitious, and intelligent enough to make decisions? I say this because all of the information and experience is out there for you to take charge and absorb. Start something. Take some online courses on the basics of business, such as finance, leadership, practice management, leveraging debt, investing basics . . . I could go on. Some find it great to pursue an MBA or some formal course to organize the information. Others start by having conversations with people who have run a business and have the similar intention of learning more. Take the risk and learn so you can arm yourself with knowledge. Risk can be uncomfortable, but keep in mind that you aren't the only one who feels that way when learning something new.

Risk can be about starting a new business or an entrepreneurial journey. When it comes to starting a business of any sort, you are in the same boat as any other entrepreneur or person who has the same desire. For you, as a physician, it may seem riskier, but that's because you are so comfortable with your expertise in medicine. As an individual who has experienced years of education and training you actually have a head start because you have already proven to yourself that you are intelligent, credible, and capable— don't forget that! In addition, starting a business or even selling a product is easier and cheaper than it has ever been. This is due to technology, available services, and the increased popularity of entrepreneurship that makes it accessible to start. Succeeding in business will always be a challenge, but the good news is that getting started (a huge step in itself) is currently easier and more affordable than ever before. Take advantage of the opportunity that is right in front of you.

Risk can also be investing capital in various opportunities outside of your income. I believe physicians are presented with great opportunities to create wealth outside of medicine, but, unfortunately, the physician community tends to be a big target for financial professionals. Being a target for having capital can bring a lot of distractions and bad deals to the table. I have experienced and seen this occur around me, where physicians are taken advantage of in investment deals. From a sales perspective, it is a dream to get in contact with a physician, as we are considered good high-net-worth individuals that may bite on an offer or product. That being said, this should not stop physicians from learning more about various opportunities and leaning on trusted sources to help them navigate passive income opportunities. Passive income is when money flows in regular intervals without the need to put in a considerable amount of effort to create it. We all want to have this scenario, but it takes some time and effort to ensure the opportunity is credible and that it is the right one for your goals and needs.

KNOW YOUR VALUE

HOW MUCH HAVE YOU ALREADY INVESTED IN YOURSELF IN ORDER TO get into this position? We can not forget that just to become a physician we have already proven ourselves to ourselves and to others. We worked our asses off to get good grades, to get a seat in medical school, to get a spot in residency . . . to pass all these challenging tests. And we did all this while trying to knock on the next door. We were trying to lead the healthcare teams around us by example, as a healer and helper of people. We have done more for ourselves and for others than most people will do over the course of a lifetime. Is this a cause to celebrate? No. This is a validation that you should not doubt yourself. This is a validation to arm yourself with confidence. This is a validation that you can do anything because you have already accomplished so much. And this is a validation that you were meant to do more. Reflect on this. Hopefully, with this new perspective, you will come to the conclusion that you can do more for yourself and for others simply by knowing your value.

I have experience in different settings, which has given me the ability to assess our value in a clinical as well as in a business environment, whether with a small startup or a large corporation. I have experience going internationally to do business in East Asia, Europe, and around the United States in different scenarios. The consistent theme is an initial level of respect, credibility, and understanding for what a physician has accomplished and what they do on a daily basis. I'm just reminding you of the doors that await your knock, the people who are waiting to engage with you on a high level of trust, and the communities that are waiting for your care. The world, containing society with so many communities in different pockets, is waiting for your impact.

When you understand and know your value in society, that's when you start to utilize it. I'm not saying that you should utilize it for bragging rights or to fulfill an ego. I'm asking you to utilize this insight to overcome doubt or any obstacles that you encounter and/or must overcome. When faced with adversity, dig deep inside yourself and remind yourself of how you save peoples' lives, how you have done more training and studying to help people than anyone else, and that your capabilities are endless. Know your value, because I'm telling you many others with far fewer accomplishments and less proof are utilizing this empowering mindset to conquer their worlds.

9

GET MOVING

Physicians are intelligent, capable, and credible people in society. If you remember that you possess those traits, and are in the midst of self-doubt while setting out on a journey, you will know that you are well prepared and ready to learn new things, try new things, and create new things.

I will bring up the point from an entrepreneur's perspective. If there was a college dropout who started a company, got funding, and then failed and the startup closed its doors—some folks may applaud the effort and evaluate the positives and negatives of the intention or endeavor. Most people wouldn't question the founder, based on their having dropped out of college or having been younger than most who have embarked on such a journey. Next, let's look at a physician who starts a company and the same outcome occurs. I can imagine some of the analysis, including that the founder was a physician and perhaps it was a lack of knowledge or experience that led to the failure. If you take a step back and look at the reasons why the physician is in the spotlight to fail vs a college dropout, it appears that being a specialist in something may take away one's ability to do generalist things. Whatever the optics are, don't believe the hype. Know your value, and make sure others know that value as you embark on your next journey.

A Physician Underdog Overcomes

OVER THE COURSE OF THE LAST YEAR, *I HAVE TALKED TO WOMEN AND minorities in medicine on a daily basis. Many are frustrated, don't see a path to leadership, aren't heard in their systems, and are feeling burned out. Many individuals have decided to leave medicine altogether, instead of continuing to go through the emotional warfare of our most current challenge, COVID 19. The healthcare system is made up of people who are amazing, caring, and intelligent individuals. They take care of patients at 2 am, on Christmas Day, Birthdays . . . all at the expense of time they could be spending with their loved ones.*

However, doctors are people that need to feel like what they are doing is valued. In the wake of COVID, we are seeing an awakening to the great divide that exists in healthcare. Physicians have lost their voice at the negotiating tables. The terms of pay, work, and patient care are often dictated by systems and outside organizations.

In medicine, we still see women re-reimbursed at rates that are lower than men in the same specialty. OBGYN is the lowest-paid surgical specialty, and it is the direct result of women's work and healthcare being undervalued. Physicians aren't able to get coverage for some needed women's medications. Women are in the minority of leadership positions, they aren't often CEOs, and they aren't at the table making decisions that impact women's health.

During my career, as a woman in medicine, advocate, and OBGYN, I have been underestimated with everything I have tried to accomplish. I had an undergraduate teacher that thought she was doing me a favor and told me how I wouldn't be able to make it in medicine because I was too soft, too emotional, and cared too much. I used that as a compliment—we need passionate and caring individuals in healthcare.

When I was growing up I was encouraged to go into different areas of medicine. I had teachers in Wisconsin tell me I would likely be more comfortable as a nurse. My father-in-law heard what I was majoring in and simply said that I shouldn't bother going into medicine, that I would likely "get pregnant and fail out." I have been told: "You're too tall; it's intimidating," "Your laugh is too loud," "You're too outgoing . . . it comes across as flirty," "Other women won't like you if you're friends with men," "Know your place, fall in line," "You will be punished for not following the hierarchy," "Wear more makeup, you look tired," "No one wants an ugly doctor," "You're just another lazy fat woman who will likely quit, and live off her husband," and so on. I have been lied about, and have had my career threatened. I have been made to feel worthless so that someone else could feel bigger.

I am still here, and I am still fighting to change the culture of medicine. And, when I am told that I am one person, and can't make any changes, I smile, because I know I have already made meaningful changes nationally. I view being underestimated as my superpower. When you work as hard as I have, to get to where I am, there isn't anything that will stop you.

KELLIE LEASE STECHER M.D.

TURNING YOUR INTENTION INTO A PLAN IS A GREAT FIRST STEP. LET'S say you would like to start a side business, and you have no idea how to even sell a product. You have a huge network of people that you already know, whether it be your cousin who you really never understood or an uncle who always seems to be busy with his work. Ask these folks—whom you have never really relied upon—ask them questions and seek information on how to start something new, and see where the conversations take you. There is more brain trust and experience in your circle of family and friends than you realize. This sounds so simple, but if you have the intention and start thinking and saying "I want to start this" instead of "I would love to start this," it can produce real movement. Reaching out to someone outside of your friend circle is another step to take. Look up a person who is selling something, whether in a brick-and-mortar store or online. Reach out to them. Tell them what you want to get started and see if they have any ideas. Is there a chance you won't get good information or that person doesn't have the time to explain it to you? Of course, but by starting to reach out to people outside of your circle, you are breaking some psychological barriers that have been placed. One step at a time and one call or meeting at a time is how businesses are built.

Having the intention to move forward is the best chance of getting through. Utilizing the mindset of awareness, taking risks, and knowing your value should be incorporated into your intention for real change to happen. It must happen for *you*—first and foremost. It must be something that moves you forward into a plan. This is how personal growth occurs. Once your momentum of growth initiates, you will be able to spread that energy to others. Once a community of empowered people is built, we can start, as an industry, to be more effective as a whole. We will have a clearer ability to make positive changes. We will continue on this journey, and affect the next generation of physicians and thereafter.

 Positive thinking is powerful thinking. If you want happiness, fulfillment, success and inner peace, start thinking you have the power to achieve those things. Focus on the bright side of life and expect positive results.

— GERMANY KENT, AUTHOR, PRINT, AND BROADCAST JOURNALIST

THE PHYSICIAN MINDSET

THE PHYSICIAN MINDSET IS SOMETHING THAT I SPEAK ABOUT frequently. The existing mindset of those in the medical field is to focus on education and the knowledge of medicine. We need to be experts in the field that we have chosen. This requires all of our time and effort. For most, it is extremely challenging to even get to the end of residency and to move on to a first job. Many of us have our learning curves and eventually settle into a comfortable routine in which we observe what others are doing in and outside of our field. Many physicians don't have influence over (or ownership of) the various tools, places, or even the people around them, and they are excluded from making high-level decisions. This can be frustrating, and it can make physicians feel out of control. I see it happening and have overheard conversations among physicians in which they express that they feel that they are workers in a system that they haven't built. I will rephrase this: Physicians work in a system that wasn't built by them or for them. Do you think that helps explain why there is an inevitable underdog scenario brewing?

IT STARTS WITH YOU

IN SHARING MY STORY AND WHAT WE AS INDIVIDUALS CAN DO, I WANT to talk a little bit about our group as a collective. In the end, if we get more momentum by knowing our value, and how we can positively impact the healthcare industry and society in general, we can move forward and be the influencers that we know we are capable of being. Personally, when my mind was able to get some breathing room, I revisited the purpose of being a physician and being a healthcare provider. It really goes to the simple concept of helping people that are sick, educating people on their health, and empowering people to seek and get help when needed. Physicians help mold the lives of many, and if we aren't doing that, it's time to restart, rebuild, disrupt . . . whatever you want to call it. I can tell you that in the world of venture, where I now live, we are reaching our goals through education, we are achieving through venture capital and investing, and we are bringing entrepreneurship to everyone who is receptive. This is what we are doing at SmileMD. We are questioning the large medical centers that are getting more specialized and farther away from the basic needs of the people. I feel we need every physician to go through this exercise and revisit what healthcare should be.

When going through exercises in building companies in various industries or investing in early-stage companies, I start by considering the problem they are trying to solve and why it has presented itself. Recently, I have found that there are many anti-quated systems that no longer serve their original purpose. If you look at college and how expensive it is, and how society and employers put pressure on us to reach that milestone, and then see so many college degrees that don't get a job but instead carry a lot of debt . . . it makes you think. If investment firms focus only on numbers and profits, it can drive the behavior of founders and companies to go in different directions, instead of perhaps solving the real problems. If you look at a political structure that was meant to govern people for safety, security, and to ensure freedom, then is that what the focus is on for the majority of the political discussions and meetings at the highest level? Unfortunately, no. These are the questions that go through the mind of an entrepreneur who is interested in not wasting time and resources, but rather would like to address the many problems seen in the world.

 It's challenging, it's not hopeless. You have to come up with something. You have to figure out a way to help them, because people must have hope to live.

— MALCOLM GLADWELL, *DAVID AND GOLIATH: UNDERDOGS,*
MISFITS, AND THE ART OF BATTLING GIANTS (BACK BAY BOOKS,
2015)

When I began practicing medicine, I would walk into the hospital without any awareness of how many people couldn't get there. I didn't realize how many people in my medical system weren't being treated because of distance, access, insurance, logistics, or even education on how to seek care. Since moving into this new career path, I have been out and engaged in the community more than I ever was previously. I employ people, I meet people, I make friends. My network and circle have expanded dramatically. I have met so many people who don't have health insurance and need help, need a physician to see for the first time or are just trying to get access to care for their family members. And I am seeing this outside of my previously narrow view as a physician. This is what is motivating me to share what I am doing today. I am seeing and experiencing what physicians can do outside of their busy clinical jobs.

When you walk into your practice, your mind from then on is on your patients for the day, the paperwork and billing that needs to be done, the oversight of staff and HR management, patient non-clinical needs, and all of the administrative duties. It makes you wonder how much time you are actually spending on bringing your expertise and services to those whose lives are in your hands? Do they even know that your practice has so many moving parts? How much time do you honestly have to speak with other physicians and/or people of influence on how your practice, or even the whole medical system, can better serve the community? How much time is spent on the learning and teaching students financial literacy, mental health wellness, nutrition, and other ways to influence people's lives, all while utilizing the expertise and experience that you have as a physician. This should be in your daily and weekly routine: question yourself and the field of medicine. Why am I not armed with ways to get involved and impact society for the better? I am not talking about lobbying groups, or bureaucratic organizations that collect money to help influence a group that in turn influences another group, etc., etc. I am talking about your voice directly impacting change. This is how we need to start thinking, what we need to start discussing, and eventually what we need to act upon as a collective. There is no time to waste, no energy left for deaf ears, no people that can tell you to hold on, and no voice more important than yours. You are an educated, competent, credible, and respected member of society who has dedicated his/her life to helping people, and there is no obstacle that should stop you from making a change. Make shit happen. Unlearn some things that organizations have taught you on how to "get involved" or how to "relieve burnout," or how to "become a leader." Instead, revisit your purpose and your potential impact.

 We really all should be entrepreneurs. People often mistake entrepreneurship as a career path, when it is truly a mindset to find fulfillment with taking action towards making something better for the world. All are capable of taking an action to create, invest, or advocate into something that makes things better for others.

— RYAN RETCHER, SENIOR PARTNER AND CHIEF OPERATING OFFICER AT LOUD CAPITAL

Entrepreneurship has empowered me to know that one person can change the world but it requires a purpose, an intention, and a strategy. Give yourself time to think, to revisit the reality of the world in which you are living, and how you want to spend your time in this life helping people. Don't think about your job or the career that has been created for you as a physician. Rather, think about how your physician skills and mindset can directly help people. When there is a public disagreement on anything medical that may be shaping people as far as their health, ensure you or one of your colleagues are represented. The non-physician participants who are included in the discussion have the drive, the risk tolerance, and the intention to be there, and we, as physicians and entrepreneurs, would be letting ourselves down if we didn't give ourselves permission to embrace the opportunity to speak and represent our interests and beliefs. Let's do that. Let's strategically align, as the ethical members of society that we are, and find ways to impact the world we care enormously about. No one else has done what we have done. This isn't a statement of ego, it's a statement of responsibility. It's a statement of driving yourself in a similar manner as you did during training, to keep training, keep impacting, and keep influencing society for the better. Realize that the world needs you. It has been calling on all of us for a long time, and it's time to respond in the manner we know we should.

MEDICAL EDUCATION

I HAVE TO SAY THAT AS I HAVE BEEN WRITING THIS BOOK, I HAVE BEEN on a path of self-discovery. I have learned more about myself, and more about my career so far, and how it occurred. In thought, I keep going back to medical school, where the true start of physician-focused learning occurred. I can now see all of the opportunities that were out there for me to learn a broader array of subjects outside of my medical focus. Medical school can and should exist to build a solid foundation for future physicians. In the current system, physicians are taught everything medical, including the fundamentals of medicine, ethics, and decision making. As with any educational institution, there are some needed changes and adaptations required in order to adjust to the changing environment and varied societal expectations. The future of medicine can be much broader in impact and more relevant to the fast-changing world around us. A really big challenge is taking all of the information and responsibilities that medical students get in their four years of school, and then see what still "needs" to be retained in the curriculum vs replaced with other educational pursuits. The opportunity is for a medical school to be more than a creator of healers, but a creator of future leaders.

 Leadership is not about a title or a designation. It's about impact, influence, and inspiration.

— Robin S. Sharma, Canadian writer and leadership expert

What do some of the best leaders have in common? They have empathy. And what is expected from physicians with regards to having empathy? Physicians are expected to be human alongside the people they care for. Be smart enough to handle the medical aspect, empathetic enough to handle the human aspect, and do both consistently over time while seeing each patient. The expectations that are placed on us should be taken as a privilege, but after acknowledging that we are human and that is how we are expected to behave, we must be brave enough to sometimes cave.

A Physician Underdog Overcomes

What is my underdog story? As a physician, the expectation that surrounds me is that I 'understand' what someone is going through. The assumption from hospital administrators, bosses, family/friends, and most importantly from patients is that we, as physicians and healers, can

empathize with a medical scenario and patient. But the truth is that we physicians may not have the slightest clue of what the patient or family is really feeling and experiencing. That to me is the number one shortcoming of our profession and leads us to be physician underdogs.

Sympathy is understanding someone else's suffering. A patient going through chemo for cancer? Yes . . . I understand that the patient is feeling nauseous, depressed, and facing death. Empathy is a whole different thing. What is empathy? Empathy cannot be taught in medical school. A physician can not read about empathy and become empathetic. Empathy is achieved through experiencing someone else's suffering. There is an emotional component where you really need to feel and experience what someone is going through that creates empathy.

We as physicians will always be underdogs. If there is an assumption that we have empathy towards patients and scenarios when we really don't, it affects the way we deliver care. This in turn affects how we thrive and succeed as physicians, and that affects every interaction we have with patients and families. It affects your resiliency, job satisfaction, and so on.

LET ME PROVIDE A LIFE-CHANGING EXAMPLE THAT I EXPERIENCED . . .

AS A JUNIOR PEDIATRIC ANESTHESIOLOGIST, MY CHILD CAME TO THE ER where I practiced as a physician. She was only three months old at the time, and she was our first child. She became profoundly dehydrated, in fact on the border of hypovolemic shock, in a very short period. When my wife called me and stated she was in the ER, I quickly had a colleague cover my operating rooms and I ran down to the first floor. I saw my child lying there, limp and lethargic. We didn't know the cause, but after multiple attempts at an IV, we eventually started providing hydration. My wife asked me if she would be admitted, and if so, would it just be overnight. I looked at her and told her we were lucky that our daughter was alive, and we would be there for a while.

I spent the next three weeks in a newly defined "dual role." I spent the days as a perceived confident healer, taking care of my patients to the best of my ability, convincing the families that I would get their three-day-old newborn through life-threatening surgery and that I understood the anxiety they were feeling. Meanwhile, I was scared shitless on the inside about my own child just three floors up in the hospital. I would spend the evenings as a nervous father, lying on an air mattress next to my three-month-old child who had IVs, PICC lines, and NG tubes, while the doctors (my very own friends and colleagues) were trying to figure out what was going on. I had my own pediatric anesthesia fellow (the same one I yelled at while asking questions/teaching in the operating room earlier that day) come and perform an anesthesia preoperative history/physical the night before my daughter had to go down for a procedure.

I spent the next day worried sick as a father, and as a physician, while my child had to undergo general anesthesia for a procedure. I felt that visceral sensation in my gut of anxiety and 'what-if's.' Soon after the procedure, things started turning around. She improved with time and eventually was discharged after three weeks of an inpatient stay. I learned a lot during those three weeks. I learned about our healthcare system. I learned about being on the other side, as well as about what it takes to be an empathetic physician.

No, I am not saying that we all need to experience an ill family member on the brink of death to learn how to be empathetic. BUT, I firmly believe, that there are immense expectations placed on us as physicians that force us to become an underdog. Use the experiences we have at work. Use the experiences outside of work. Use the experiences with family and friends. Stay humble and continuously learn. By having a better consideration of empathy and building on our experiences and interactions, we can be better physicians and humans.

TARUN BHALLA M.D.

MEDICAL SCHOOL WAS WHAT MANY OF US HAD WORKED HARD TO GET into and was a goal for many others. Once we were in, there was an intense and, of course, necessary learning of all things medical. With many physicians facing the obstacles I listed earlier in this book, I would like to see more subjects introduced to students that would enable them to pursue their broader journey earlier on their paths. Perhaps there could be more emphasis on this skill set rather than on just memorizing content. By skill set, I am referring to qualities that include financial literacy, mental and physical wellness, nutrition, and leadership and management in the workplace. How can the medical school curriculum be shaped so that the broader qualities of their students are optimized and their impact in and outside of the field is more in mind? Understandably, there is a lot to cover in four years to produce a physician capable and ready to pursue a residency or other paths, but does that time have to be devoted to only all things medical? The opportunity is for a medical school to be more than a creator of healers, but a creator of future leaders. Future leaders that have a physician foundation will have the medical skills necessary to take care of patients clinically, have the financial literacy to responsibly manage their own personal and business finances, have the knowledge and motivation to maintain physical health and mental wellness, have a great foundation on nutrition and what it means for themselves and for the people around them, and have leadership skills to manage people and be as impactful as possible. These are some of the skill sets that I would like to see introduced in the foundation of medical school. By looking at the goal of medical school more broadly, perhaps we in the field can accomplish more and become more impactful. The theme of this book is to open the minds of physicians to the opportunities outside of medical school, through which they can impact society more broadly. I feel medical schools should include a wider range of instruction that could help students prepare for the responsibilities and pressures that they, as physicians, have ahead of them. I will list a few ideas to help brainstorm ways we can improve our medical education.

A PHYSICIAN UNDERDOG OVERCOMES

I think like a lot of us, it's hard to call myself an underdog based on where I am in life now, especially as so many around the world struggle just to keep a job. But I need to remember all those times where my life story didn't seem so promising or go as planned.

Back in high school, I had done well as an athlete. However, I got denied by multiple big-name colleges (Ivy League) and in my mind had to settle for my state university—Strike 1. In college, I struggled my first year and left premed for a while because of my grades. I had to learn that becoming a doctor might not be in my future despite my desire to be one—Strike 2. After med school, I had set my mind on certain residency programs. I luckily got a spot but only on my fourth choice. I didn't feel so lucky at the time—Strike 3.

I used to feel inadequate because the expectations I had for myself didn't work out as I had planned. This made me feel like I didn't belong at times. What I have realized, though, is that those unexpected scenarios actually gave me strength. It's easy to keep grinding and moving forward when things go your way, but the real test is to use those unexpected scenarios to show you who you really are. I think all of us feel like underdogs at times, but it's our tenacity and perseverance that make us one no longer.

AJAY SATYAPRIYA M.D.

NAVIN GOYAL M.D.

Should we learn leadership skills so when we enter society we are more prepared for the stage? Should we also know this to manage people around us in the medical environment and in society? Should we learn basic finance to be able to manage our own finances, while also preparing us for any future practices in which we work? Should we learn about self-care and how important it is for us to be sustainable and thrive? From mental wellness, physical wellness, nutrition, sleep, and the many things we use to educate and guide our patients, do we have the foundation to help ourselves? Should we learn about people's lack of access to the health care we are learning, and how we as physicians can help in solving this problem? If we don't know the problems, we can't help solve them. Should we? If we keep asking questions and have enough curiosity to follow up and have discussions to learn more, could we really start changing the world?

Another consideration is the route medical students take in order to just get into school. Many of us spend an average of four years in college prior to attending medical school. I am beyond questioning this process or route, but I am revisiting the question of what is best for future physicians—will they be utilizing their education and ethics in order to help people and society in general? Does it make sense to attend college for four years to learn a general curriculum of content while waiting to get into the field you feel is the best for you? Does it make sense to work really hard to get grades to prove yourself worthy of medical school, only to be inundated with four more years of content in order to be able to train in a hospital? I do have some thoughts but I definitely don't have the answers. I am not trying to repave a path that many of us have already taken or are already on our way through. Rather, just like the healthcare system that I have questioned multiple times throughout this book, I want to question the future of our training and the ability of our medical field to thrive. If we don't question it we are simply putting bandaids on a large wound. I feel a strong responsibility to question what we can do better, and explore how we can optimize our time and focus, and

136

how we can prepare ourselves for the changes that have already begun in this decade.

I don't want this book to convey any disappointment in the field of medicine; I am very proud of my medical background. Instead, I would rather present the idea that there are opportunities out there that can improve the trajectory of our lives, and capitalize on our capabilities. This new mindset is one that is fruitful and provides a more comprehensive path to fulfillment. I am in a unique position to invest and push for change in numerous industries, but I feel that focusing on the many bright minds in the medical field is a great start. I have taken a lot of risks to be where I am and, to tell you the truth, it is liberating and fulfilling to be in my current position. I am several years into my entrepreneurial journey, but I am aware that there is a lot more that we need to do in the true form of Venture For People ™. Just remember that if you are reading or listening to this book, you already have a hunger or drive to do more. One action or step by you can create a whole new direction for yourself and for others.

 But so much of what is beautiful and valuable in the world comes from the shepherd, who has more strength and purpose than we ever imagine.

— MALCOLM GLADWELL, *DAVID AND GOLIATH: UNDERDOGS, MISFITS, AND THE ART OF BATTLING GIANTS* (BACK BAY BOOKS, 2015)

As I mentioned at the beginning of this book, the underdog is intriguing to me. I feel underdogs have always been associated with the less favored, the ones who had to face larger challenges than others, or someone that had traits that automatically put them in a category to be bet against the odds. Physicians are underdogs. Once you acknowledge this underdog scenario, you are able to take a step back and look at what your expectations were and where they are now. This acknowledgment is the first step to taking real action—not by feeling sorry for yourself but rather by being energized to utilize your underdog mentality. There are advantages to being an underdog and one shouldn't hesitate to lean on those advantages when trying to push in a direction that is more favorable. Favorable can snowball from being bet against into being bet on.

It's been a pleasure not only to write these thoughts and brainstorm how we as a collective can impact more broadly but also to encourage others to find the time and mindset to think. I hope, at the least, this has opened some energy or ideas to take what we have in front of us and mold it into something greater. Remember, we all start from somewhere, and my start was at a kitchen table. If you want to be at a particular table, do what you need to get there. If you can't get to where you want to be, build a table. If anyone tries to stop you, even if it's you stopping you, don't give up and keep trying. It's literally those steps that I expect to face every day now and it's those actions that keep me moving forward. Best of luck on your journey, and don't forget to discuss more, brainstorm more, observe more, share more stories and ideas, and always . . . always . . . always move forward.

A Physician Underdog Overcomes

Real change for physicians could be lifesaving for society. This sounds like a bold statement, but physicians aren't just healers in society, they are leaders, they are credible and ethical role models, and they have the ability to help shape a society that promotes health and humanity. Real change for physicians will not be pretty, easy, or smooth. Real

*change requires looking in the mirror, and then looking outside of medi-
cine and observing what caregivers and those being cared for perceive how
physicians are contributing to the world. My perspective, especially after
leaving the practice of medicine and running a business that empowers
entrepreneurs and problem-solvers, has been evolving.*

NAVIN GOYAL M.D.

RECOMMENDED RESOURCES

These are books and other resources that I have personally read or listened to. I feel they are inspirational, motivational, and informative and can broaden your mindset. I especially enjoy reading about other people's stories and believe that they could be helpful as you expand, explore, and learn new skills. There is also an online platform that I helped start in an effort to encourage physicians to apply what they have learned and grow as more comprehensive individuals. The platform is called *Beyond Physician* and if you are a medical student or a physician, please visit www. beyondphysician.com

These are the materials that taught me something while transitioning from medical professional to entrepreneur, and even now being in a leadership position for multiple organizations. They taught me something that I feel may be valuable to others. They encouraged me to learn and grow and become a more complete person. I hope you continue your learning journey and become the best version of yourself. These resources along with others can be found at www.physicianunderdog.com.

Books:

1. *Range* by David Epstein (Macmillan Publishers, 2019)
2. *Good to Great: Why Some Companies Make the Leap and Others Don't* by Jim Collins (HarperBusiness, 2001)
3. *Elon Musk: Tesla, SpaceX, and the Quest for a Fantastic Future* by Ashlee Vance (HarperCollins, 2015)
4. *Steve Jobs: The exclusive biography* by Walter Isaacson (Simon & Schuster, 2011)
5. *Shantaram* by Gregory David Roberts (Scribe Publications [Australia], 2003)
6. *Unbroken: A World War II Story of Survival, Resilience, and Redemption* by Laura Hillenbrand (Penguin Random House LLC, 2010)
7. *The Ride of a Lifetime: Lessons Learned from 15 years as CEO of Walt Disney Company* by Robert Iger (Penguin Random House, 2019)
8. *Shoe Dog: A Memoir by the Creator of Nike* by Phil Knight (Simon & Schuster, 2016)
9. *David and Goliath: Underdogs, Misfits, and the Art of Battling Giants* by Malcolm Gladwell (Little, Brown & Company, 2013)
10. *The Subtle Art of Not Giving a F*ck* by Mark Manson (HarperCollins Publishers, 2016)

When it comes to visual representations on entrepreneurship and resilience, I co-authored an infographic that highlights certain markets that are more resilient than others and displays how downturns can spark innovation, leadership, and more. This infographic can be found at: http://loud.vc/recession-resilience-infographic/

As far as podcasts, I have only steered toward one. After trying many that I thought kept me engaged and taught me something, I realized that a podcast has a low barrier to entry. It takes effort to have a focused strategy and plan, it takes effort to record with quality intention and editing, and it takes effort to engage the audience and bring interesting guests on. I say this because the only one to date that I find entertaining, educational, and keeps me interested and engaged is *How I Built This with Guy Raz* from NPR.

ACKNOWLEDGMENTS

This book was created through the inspiration and support I received from many people. As I mentioned in the book, along my path there have been many people who have contributed to my journey, some that I have to definitely mention. I want to thank my wife, Mili, for being just herself, a loving wife and mother, and for being my partner through this life-changing journey, and for all the love and foundational support she has given me and our family. I also want to thank her for being an intelligent and empathetic physician who is passionate about her work and continues to help so many patients. You are a great role model for our kids and the nieces and nephews who all have observed and been inspired by you.

I want to thank my two daughters, Raina and Asha, for being sweet, curious, and extremely excited as I have been writing and producing this book. They were supportive during my change in careers, and they experienced the voyage along with me. I look at the world through their eyes and am reminded of how beautiful and simple life should be. I want them to be proud to be who they are and whoever they will become. A lot of this book is speaking directly to them.

I want to thank my sister Sapna for her huge support when

growing up, and for being a responsible adult when I wasn't. I want to thank my sister Renita for helping her little brother grow up, and for being a friend when one was needed. To be in the same geographical area, to experience all we have in life, and to you both being cool aunts to my kids, I can't help but acknowledge how extremely lucky we are to have each other. A special shoutout to my nieces and nephews who also remind me to be better, that my actions are speaking to everyone, and to always laugh when the family is around.

I want to thank my mom for being so supportive and loving since day one, and my dad for being a role model for me and the whole family. My parents supported me emotionally, financially, and sacrificed so much on their end to get me to where I am today. I hope to be the same supportive and foundational parent as they were.

I want to thank my unofficial brother, Sonny, who has been my best friend since we were babies. I appreciate the support and encouragement he has offered throughout all my adventures. You helped me understand the amount of work that goes into a business and realize the amount of fulfillment and joy that can result from these endeavors. A special thanks to my aunts and uncles, family members, and family friends, for upholding a strong Indian community and culture when I was growing up, which in turn provided and still provides a level of support and a solid foundation that I never imagined.

For the journey of starting SmileMD and just navigating life as an elementary student, I want to thank my brothers Tarun and Ajay. It's tough to find friends who become family, and it's even tougher to start a company together, but I'm grateful to you both for balancing me as a person. I learned more about myself, learned more about others, and as a result sought to be a better person. My other childhood brother Srikar, who reads people like it's his sixth sense, has provided me with a deep friendship that is empowering. He has repeatedly shown me what true brotherhood entails. Between Tarun, Ajay, Srikar, and myself, we have a HOME TEAM that has only gotten closer, more special, and more meaningful as we navigate this journey called life.

When it comes to my journey as a partner developing LOUD Capital, I want to thank my brother in business Darshan for motivating me, reminding me that I can do anything, and helping me navigate the crazy world of venture in a company that we were building from scratch. I remember the dialogue we had while I was still practicing clinically, and your investment of time into those conversations armed me to move forward. We have started a snowball of adventures that keep coming our way and I wouldn't want to be a Yang to anyone else's Ying. I want to thank Ryan Retcher for being a really good friend and for representing the empathetic foundation that drives our organization. We have experienced a lot together, all the way back to the early years of SmileMD and LOUD Capital, and I'm glad we are together on this journey to see how we can impact the world from our common mission. I want to thank Nishad for being a great friend, one who can sell effectively and persuade genuinely, and who is a constant reminder to me that anything is possible. Your professionalism, your discipline, and your experience have been extremely helpful and motivating. I want to thank Ethan for his wisdom and encouragement that have helped me lead this special group. It's not common to grow a friendship across the globe, but we have proven that it can happen and that it can thrive. I have to thank my man, Marshall, for being a genuine, hard-working fellow physician who has given me great advice and friendship and believed in me early on. Your belief in the organization that we have been building means more than you know. You are on a journey similar to the one that I have been on, and I know you will get exactly what you have been working so hard for (but I know that you know this already). My LOUD partner Brian, who is one of the smartest guys I know, has taught me so much and has been a real friend. I have truly enjoyed our philosophical discussions. Thanks for believing I could actually write a book. If we ever make it really big and they do a story on us, you will be credited for calling the

LOUD team the SUPER GROUP, believing we were badasses individually and came together to form a super talented team! For Wolf Starr, the guy who is full of empathy and whose mantra to support local businesses gave me real-life examples on how to be good to people: thank you for bringing people and community to anything venture and entrepreneurship. I know your plan to positively influence LOUD and venture has been effective. Thank you to the whole LOUD Capital team, which is composed of many folks not mentioned above, but a group of investors, companies, and stakeholders who inspire and encourage me to do better, think bigger and make this so much more than a career.

I want to thank the team that specifically helped with this book. This book specifically was edited by Anne McNamara. I appreciate her input, and especially for reading and editing the content as it was being freshly created! I am a new author and it takes a special amount of patience to have worked on this project. I want to thank Adam Lehman for designing a creative and impactful book cover. And I want to thank Niraj Shekhar for taking the time to photograph and edit the photos of myself, one being on the back cover.

There are many people in my life that have indirectly or even directly impacted this book who I have not mentioned, but I appreciate the family, friendship, and community it takes to motivate one another and to continue sharing our learnings whenever possible. If you have made it this far, you are the first one here. Congratulations!